Teaching the
Selected Works of
Gary Paulsen

The Young Adult Novels in the Classroom Series

When former Heinemann–Boynton/Cook editor Peter Stillman first conceived the Young Adult Literature (YAL) series in 1990 and asked me to be the series editor, I was excited to be part of such an innovative endeavor. At that time there were few professional books available for teachers who wanted to bring young adult literature into their classrooms, and Heinemann was the first publisher making a concerted effort to fill this need. Seventeen years and many books later, under the direction of Heinemann Executive Editor Lisa Luedeke, the series continues to inform and assist teachers at the middle school, high school, and college levels as they read with and teach to their students the best works that the field of young adult literature has to offer.

The Heinemann YAL series takes another step forward with the book you hold in your hands. This subseries on teaching the works of specific young adult authors is designed to help you incorporate young adult literature into your curriculum, providing ideas and lessons that you may use and offering examples of classroom-tested student work, lesson plans, and discussion as an impetus to designing your own lessons and developing your own ideas in accordance with your students' needs.

Over the years, many teachers in my graduate young adult literature classes have asked me how to convince administrators and parents that young adult literature is worthy of a place in the curriculum alongside the classics and other commonly taught literary works. In response I have shown them how to write rationales for specific books, how to design lesson plans and units that satisfy state and national standards, how to deal with censorship, and how to become connoisseurs of young adult literature themselves. I hope that the books in this subseries, by focusing on specific authors of young adult literature and highlighting the successful work of teachers with this genre, will inspire confidence in you to bring these extraordinary works into your curriculum, not just as a bridge to the classics, but as literary works in their own right.

—Virginia R. Monseau

Teaching the Selected Works of Robert Cormier

Teaching the Selected Works of Mildred D. Taylor

Teaching the Selected Works of Katherine Paterson

Teaching the Selected Works of Walter Dean Myers

Teaching the Selected Works of Chris Crutcher

Teaching the Selected Works of Gary Paulsen

Teaching the Selected Works of Gary Paulsen

Gary M. Salvner
Youngstown State University

HEINEMANN
PORTSMOUTH, NH

Heinemann
361 Hanover Street
Portsmouth, NH 03801–3912
www.heinemann.com

Offices and agents throughout the world

© 2009 by Gary M. Salvner

Library of Congress Cataloging-in-Publication Data
 Teaching the selected works of Gary Paulsen / Gary M. Salvner.
  p. cm. — (Young adult novels in the classroom)
 Includes bibliographical references.
 ISBN-13: 978-0-325-00988-9
 ISBN-10: 0-325-00988-0
 1. Paulsen, Gary—Study and teaching. 2. Young adult literature,
American—Study and teaching. I. Title.

PS3566.A834Z86 2009
813'.54—dc22   2009012598

Editor: Virginia R. Monseau
Production: Vicki Kasabian
Cover design: Night & Day Design
Typesetter: Tom Allen, Pear Graphic Design
Manufacturing: Steve Bernier

Printed in the United States of America on acid-free paper
13 12 11 10 09 VP 1 2 3 4 5

For three master teachers—
Gail Barnhart, Meg Silver, and Christa Welch—and for
Gary Paulsen

CONTENTS

＊

*If I could say anything to teachers and librarians who put books, any
books, in the hands of kids, it would be this: Thank you.
Thank you for every time you come across a "bad" student who is a
"poor" reader and you don't let that stop you from finding a book,
one book, the book that will interest that kid. I was that kid,
and one woman, a librarian in Minnesota, took the time to find a book for me.
In a very real way, I owe everything I am to that one gesture.*

&

Gary Paulsen

ACKNOWLEDGMENTS

I am grateful to three dedicated teachers who helped with this project by using novels by Gary Paulsen in their classrooms and keeping track of the results. Gail Barnhart, a seventh-grade language arts teacher at Crestview Middle School in Columbiana, Ohio, had her students read *Hatchet* and the other Brian books and recorded their thoughtful insights about the survival theme in the stories. Margaret Silver, who teaches at Southside Middle School in Columbiana, Ohio, began her reading/writing workshop year with a whole-class examination of *The Monument*, finding ample connections between the experiences of Rocky Turner and Mick Strum in the novel and her own students' efforts to become skilled readers and writers. Christa Welch, a tenth-grade teacher at Sharon High School in Sharon, Pennsylvania, had one of her classes read *The Crossing*, followed by a literature circle exploration of three other multicultural titles by Paulsen, and she attentively tracked their observations throughout the unit. I could not have completed this work without the cooperation, dedication, and skill of these three outstanding educators.

I also thank Jennifer Flannery, Gary Paulsen's literary agent, for providing information and putting me back in touch with Gary Paulsen; the Youngstown State University (YSU) Research Council for partially funding classroom book sets; and YSU's Dean Shearle Furnish and Provost Ikram Khawaja for supporting the project with reassigned time and encouragement.

Finally, and always, I thank my wife, Kathy—for patience, good humor, and love.

Gary Paulsen—Writer and Adventurer

Who Is Gary Paulsen?

Over a writing career of forty-plus years, Gary Paulsen has published more than 200 books, a staggering total given the effort required of writing and the time Paulsen has also invested in outdoor adventures such as dogsledding and sailing. His motivation for doing so is simply described, however. "I write because I have a story to tell," Paulsen explains, "because I love the way words dance on the page. I write because I cannot *not* write" (email correspondence 2008).

The purpose of this book is to examine how selected works of this prolific and award-winning author of young adult novels might be taught effectively in middle and high school classrooms, and a beginning question might be how much one needs to know about Paulsen the man in order to appreciate Paulsen the writer.

"Mining my life is really what I do when I write," Gary Paulsen has said. "I don't make stuff up much. Most of the things I write about are based on personal inspection at zero altitude, and I have scars pretty much all over my body to prove those things" (Salvner

1996, 4). In both his work and his public presentations, Paulsen has been open about his difficult childhood, his parents' and his own alcoholism, his early setbacks as a writer as well as his victories. Paulsen has also talked engagingly about the adventures of his life—the thousands of miles he's logged on dogsleds, the Iditarod races, the long trips on sailboats, the canoeing and hunting journeys.

There is no doubt that Gary Paulsen's works stand on their own and can be read successfully by young people and the rest of us without autobiographical annotation, but it is equally true that something is added to the reading when one realizes that the stories of Paulsen's huge body of work are also, often, the stories of his life. And so any teaching of his books is enriched by at least a brief biography.

Gary Paulsen's Life

Who is this Gary Paulsen? He was born on May 17, 1939, in Minneapolis, Minnesota, to Eunice and Oscar Paulsen. His father went to war in Europe during World War II before Gary knew him, and Paulsen was raised by his mother, who moved to Chicago to work in a munitions plant and—on a few occasions—sent the young Gary to stay with his grandmother in northern Minnesota (events retold in stories such as *The Cookcamp* [1991]). After the war, Oscar Paulsen was transferred to the Philippines, and his wife and son went to join him there. In Manila, Gary saw his parents dissolve into alcoholism while he wandered the destroyed city on his own. Eventually the family moved back to the United States, and they resettled in Thief River Falls, Minnesota, where Gary spent most of his school years.

Those years weren't happy ones as his parents' alcoholism continued, and Gary escaped to live at times with relatives and, mostly, to the nearby woods, which became his refuge. Paulsen often tells the story of a librarian at the local library who took an interest in him after he came in one night to get out of the cold. The woman began picking out books for him to read, and he was soon hooked. Hiding out in his basement, he began reading to escape, and between books and the woods, he found a way to get through his teenage years.

After barely passing high school, Gary Paulsen tried college, joined the Army (which he hated), and eventually learned electronics and went to work in satellite tracking. One night, staring at a radar screen in California, he picked up a magazine on flying and was captivated by the power of the stories to engage him; he decided not that he wanted to fly, but that he wanted to write about what he knew. Quickly and irrationally he quit his job, moved to Hollywood and then back to Minnesota, slowly learned the craft of writing, and began to have small success as a writer. Moving to Taos, New Mexico, and meeting his wife Ruth Wright Paulsen, a local artist, Paulsen set up a life for himself. They moved to Ruth's native Colorado, where the Paulsens' son Jim was born, but sadly, soon after, Gary Paulsen lost his bearings and became afflicted with his own alcoholism. Over a period of months and years, he lost most of what he knew about writing as he worked construction and other odd jobs.

In 1973, Gary Paulsen found a way to redirect himself, and he quit drinking. Moving back to Minnesota with his wife and young son, Paulsen began relearning how to write, and he partially supported himself by trapping game for food and bounty. Having been given a broken sled and four dogs by a friend, Paulsen learned to run dogsleds to expand his trap line, but he soon grew more in love with being with his dogs on the sled than with the trapping itself.

In some ways, dogsledding gave Gary Paulsen a focus that he hadn't had before, and it seemed to have rubbed off on his writing also as he began to receive positive reviews for new works, including *Popcorn Days and Buttermilk Nights* (1983), *Dancing Carl* (1983), and *Tracker* (1984).

In 1983, Gary Paulsen entered the Iditarod dogsled race, the famed 1,200-mile race from Anchorage to Nome, Alaska, dubbed "The Last Great Race on Earth." To his own surprise and that of others (he was ranked by other mushers as the least likely to finish), he completed the entire run, finishing in forty-second place.

He entered again in 1985 and was near the finish on the edge of the Bering Sea when he was swept out onto sea ice and had to be rescued.

In the midst of this newfound love of dogs and racing, Gary Paulsen continued to write, completing three Newbery Honor Books (*Dogsong* [1985], *Hatchet* [1987], and *The Winter Room* [1989]) in the late 1980s. Then, on a book tour in 1990, Paulsen was struck with chest pains that his doctor diagnosed as a sign of significant heart problems, and Paulsen was told to give up his hard life. While in the hospital, he arranged for the sale of his entire kennel of dogs, unable to personally face the loss of them.

No longer running dogs, Gary Paulsen turned his additional energy and time into more writing, and his output became staggering. In the early to mid-1990s, he completed three to five books and a number of short series titles each year.

Paulsen took care of his health and turned to sailing the Pacific, purchasing a sailboat he named Felicity and sailing it to Fiji and Hawaii as well as along the California coast. In 2003, he learned that his heart was healthy enough that he could resume his work with dogs, and he immediately relocated to Alaska to train for further Iditarods and feel the pleasures, once more, of working with the animals that he clearly loves. He has prepared for the race a number of times in recent years, once more fully enthralled by the experience and ready, despite being in his upper sixties, to try the adventure again.

Although he maintains a ranch in New Mexico, today Gary Paulsen spends most of his time with his kennel of dogs in Willow, Alaska, near Anchorage, writing and (whenever he can) running with his dog team.

Paulsen the Writer: What to Look For

Gary Paulsen has tried virtually everything in writing—adult thrillers, nonfiction books on home repair, young adult adventure books, science fiction and humor, historical fiction, westerns, picture books, multicultural stories, memoirs and personal essays, and series titles for young readers. Yet in all of that variety, there are noticeable patterns in his work.

In teaching Paulsen's books, it makes sense to know about those patterns. An advantage of using Paulsen's work in the classroom is that the patterns are visible and common, and even fairly young readers will notice them. Furthermore, these patterns—repeating themes, character types, settings, even style—uncover some of what we might want to teach students about both the pleasures and the intricacies of good literature.

Gary Paulsen's books don't teach themselves, but they certainly can set up excellent lessons that cover many of the literature curriculum goals and standards we are obliged to address in English classes. Furthermore, they invite rich writing (both analysis and personal response) from students, who see and understand these literary elements and who also appreciate the immediacy of Paulsen's stories.

So, what are some of these patterns? The next three chapters of this book outline some of Paulsen's most prominent motifs: exploration of the theme of survival, treatment of issues of maturation and growing up, and an examination of multicultural and social justice topics. Classroom testing of Paulsen books associated with each illustrate how these patterns might be put to effective use in middle and high school classrooms.

A final chapter of this book examines other opportunities for using Gary Paulsen's works in the classroom by discussing character types, stylistic features, and other patterns that offer rich possibilities for student exploration.

Hatchet and the Brian Books
Paulsen's Tales of Survival

Any reader of Paulsen's works immediately notices how predominant the theme of survival is in them. Mostly this is survival in the natural world, like Brian Robeson's struggle to survive in northern Canada for fifty-four days in *Hatchet* (1987) and his further adventures in the other Brian books. Outdoor survival also features in the sailing story *The Voyage of the* Frog (1989); *The Haymeadow* (1992), a novel about a boy who tends sheep in the high country of Wyoming; and nonfiction works like *Caught by the Sea* (2001), *Woodsong* (1990), and *Guts* (2001).

Gary Paulsen's survival tales are remarkable in that, despite the number of them, they're rarely repetitive. Yes, many begin with the same plunge into danger followed by the same small steps in learning to hunt, fish, create lodgings and fire, but each endeavor brings new knowledge and new lessons about resilience, and so each in its own way is different. In the same way that Brian Robeson agrees to teach outdoor survival expert Derek about what he's learned in *The River* (1991), Paulsen seems to have laid out lessons to us in his various works—some about what to expect in the natural world (e.g., *Woodsong*), and some about the mind-set and skills one must develop if one hopes to survive (e.g., *The Haymeadow*).

Asked whether Brian Robeson's lessons in the Brian books constitute a pattern of development—an evolution in the character—Paulsen wrote,

> I never thought of him evolving so much as learning how to face up to whatever came his way. I have changed because of the different things I have done or experienced throughout the years (a bad childhood, the Army, being broke, running dogs, riding horses, sailing, writing) and, if Brian changed in the books, it is a direct response to what he learned, what he saw, how he had to react and adapt to survive. (email correspondence 2008)

One of the pleasures of teaching Paulsen's survival stories together is to invite students to accumulate knowledge about contending with "whatever comes [one's] way," lessons about the world and about self that make one a survivor. These lessons are many and varied, and the search for them in Paulsen's many out-in-nature works is rich, indeed.

A Unit on Survival

Gail Barnhart teaches seventh-grade language arts at Crestview Middle School, a rural district adjacent to the villages of Columbiana and New Waterford in northeastern Ohio. For this project, Gail agreed to teach a survival unit focusing on Gary Paulsen's *Hatchet* and the succeeding books about Brian Robeson, a thirteen-year-old who, in the opening book, endures a plane crash into the Canadian wilderness and survives for fifty-four days on his own determination and ingenuity.

About *Hatchet*

Hatchet, a Newbery Honor Book, is by far Gary Paulsen's most popular title, having sold more than 4.5 million copies since its publication in 1987 and having become a regular part of the curriculum in many middle school language arts classes. In the book, Brian Robeson is on his way to spend the summer with his father in the Canadian north shortly after his parents' divorce when the pilot of his small plane suffers a fatal heart attack. Brian keeps the plane flying for hours, trying unsuccessfully to get help on the radio, and when the plane finally runs out of gas, he guides it out onto an L-shaped lake where it crashes and sinks.

Brian makes it to shore, and the next morning, aware that he has survived, he begins to take stock of his situation. Brian knows almost nothing about the outdoors and has almost nothing of use with him except for a hatchet his mother had given him that is threaded onto his belt.

Initially Brian hopes for rescue, but when a plane flies by and doesn't spot his signal fire and then no planes return, he must admit that he is on his own. He comes to realize that he must seek for ways to survive.

Brian finds berries to eat, eventually makes a primitive lance and bow and, after much practice, is able to spear fish and hunt game. He makes a shelter in a hollow in a rock face alongside the lake, learns to build a fire, and slowly, through close observation and ingenious problem solving, Brian becomes a survivor. When he is attacked by animals and survives a tornado, Brian learns that self-pity does no good—that "feeling sorry for yourself didn't work. It wasn't just that it was wrong to do, or that it was considered incorrect. It was more than that—it didn't work" (82).

After nearly two months in the wild, a storm kicks the wrecked plane partly out of the water, and Brian recovers the survival pack stored in the back. Unknowingly, he activates an emergency transmitter, and a few hours later, just as he is settling down to dinner, a pilot in the area responds to the signal and lands his seaplane on the lake. Just as suddenly as Brian was tossed into the wilderness, he is rescued. The book ends with an epilogue cataloging changes in Brian once he returns to civilization and reporting what Brian learns about where he has been and what he has encountered.

An important subplot of *Hatchet* revolves around a "secret" Brian carries with him into the wilderness. Before his parents' divorce, Brian saw his mother meeting another man and giving him a kiss, and Brian burns with anger over this betrayal and wants some kind of revenge. The secret resurfaces in dreams Brian has in the woods, and at least early on, it keeps pulling Brian back from his current situation into the world he has known previously. Finally, after he is rescued, he realizes that the secret is irrelevant, and telling it will help no one.

Teaching *Hatchet*

With survival as the key theme, Gail Barnhart set up a series of lessons and class experiences for her seventh graders to enrich the reading of *Hatchet*. In the first prereading activity, Gail asked the students to define *survival* and to draw something that they thought symbolized the word. Many of the definitions were straightforward and simple, as one might expect. Luke said that survival was "to live and accomplish your goal," and Adam noted that it was to "meet the three basic needs: food, water, shelter." A few suggested additional nuances. Michael said that survival was "to make it through rough times and use the resources you have," and Matthew suggested that it was "to live through life and accomplish the things you need to do." The visual symbols students drew were also relatively simple, but a few showed interesting insights. Nathan depicted survival as the sun, explaining that the sun was the source of life (and thus of survival), and James drew a rainbow and related it to a biblical tale of survival, the story of Noah's ark.

Gail followed up these initial musings with a journal assignment in which students were asked to imagine a survival situation.

"Imagine that you are on a hiking trip," she wrote, "and you get lost deep in the woods of Beaver Creek [a wilderness state park near the school that students had visited on a field trip]. What would be your first step once you realized you were lost? How would you feel?"

Students talked about looking for shelter somewhere and about finding food. The "feelings" question elicited what one might expect—comments about fear, anxiety, and loneliness. One said, for example, "I would feel scared because of the decisions I might have to make on my own when trying to survive in the wilderness," and another thought of loneliness because "I would have no one to talk to."

Gail followed this response with a second question, asking students to write about a time when they were in danger. She reported:

> This was an awesome activity. We spent most of the period talking about dangerous situations. Some of the situations were: being rescued from a pool at the age of two, sleepwalking and ultimately being found sleeping in the snow, getting lost in the store, a near-death experience with a semi, etc. . . . Once a few students started opening up, everyone wanted to share. It was a great way to get them thinking about a dangerous situation and the fear they felt. This will help them develop empathy for Brian.

Developing empathy and awareness was exactly the aim of these opening exercises, and once they were completed, Gail dove directly into the book. She engaged students by reading the first chapter aloud, after which the class chatted briefly about Brian's situation at the beginning of the novel, including his parents' divorce. Students seemed willing to open up and explore the situation. One referred to her parents' own fighting, worrying that they, like Brian's parents, might divorce.

Having encountered the opening circumstances of the book, students were told to read Chapters 2 through 4 as homework and to record impressions in their journals as they read. Gail asked them to focus on three key words in these chapters: *flight* (the plane flight and crash); *nothing* (the final word of Chapter 3 as Brian makes it to shore and passes out); and *luck* (Brian's realization in Chapter 4 that good luck and bad luck sometimes intertwine).

As students came to class the next day, Gail set up a dialogue journal format for student interaction, in which students recorded thoughts and impressions and then exchanged journals and responded to one another's comments. The dialogue journals worked particularly well with two questions the class explored in this early session. First, Gail simply asked students, "Why did the pilot let Brian fly the plane?" and the answers showed insight and rich speculation about the situation. As Gail recorded in her notes on the session,

> Many students answered the question by suggesting that the pilot knew something was wrong, and Paulsen was foreshadowing. My favorite answers, however, focused on the pilot's act of compassion toward Brian. They suggested that the reason was because he noticed Brian was upset and wanted to cheer him up.

A second question that generated rich student interaction was "Would you keep the 'secret'? Why?" Again, student reactions showed both that they were starting to trust one another with honest responses and that they were actively empathizing with Brian. Of the responses, Gail wrote:

> The students were split as to the decision whether they would share the secret or not. Those who would share the secret believed it was the right thing to do. They said they would want to know. Those who would keep the secret said they would not want to make things worse for either parent. One or two students, however, said they would tell someone else. They realized the burden of the secret Brian was carrying. I was very proud of them for their comments!

Gail continued alternating chapters read aloud with chapters read by the students as homework. After she read Chapter 5 to them, she paused for two activities intended to connect students to the circumstances of the story at this point. In the fifth chapter, Brian has survived the crash and comes to the realization that he is stranded in the wilderness. To dampen his panic, he decides to "take stock" of what he has with him, remembering his English teacher Mr. Perpich's exhortation to "stay positive and stay on top of things" (49). So Brian takes inventory of what he has: a twenty-dollar bill and change, paper, a broken watch, a torn windbreaker, a billfold, nail clippers, the clothes he wears, and the hatchet that still hangs on the belt. Brian also remembers Mr. Perpich emphasizing to students that "You are your most valuable asset . . . the best thing you have" (51), and so he includes himself on the list.

Gail decided to have students extrapolate from that list by asking them to imagine how Brian might be able to use these items, and they came up with ingenious possibilities. The windbreaker, they speculated, might be used as a fishing net, or it might be waved as a signal flag if a rescue plane came overhead. They also imagined it being used to string up food or filter water.

Gail was also interested to have students capture the emotional circumstances at this point in the book and asked them to imagine what Brian's parents might be thinking as time went on and Brian's plane didn't arrive. Realizing that a rescue operation would be organized, students were asked to write out a missing person report on Brian that included basic physical features (name, age, sex, height, weight, hair and eye color) and information about where he was last seen and where he was going. Some designed "Have You Seen Me?" posters like those on milk cartons and billboards, and they captured the terse informational voice of such announcements. Jason's notice, for example, stated,

> ATTENTION!! This is a missing person alert. Brian Robeson, male, has gone on a small bushplane called a Cessna-406 heading to visit his dad around the Canadian Wilderness. He was last seen in Hampton, New York, in a small airport before he took off on the plane. Possible places to look for him are somewhere in the Canadian wilderness or around the oil fields in Canada and that

area. Brian Robeson is a 5 ft 2 in. male who is 13 years old and has brown hair, blue eyes, and 112 lbs.

After reading Chapters 6 and 7 for homework, students were asked to focus on two dominant themes of those chapters—hunger and home. In Chapter 6, Brian finally contends with his serious hunger and begins to find food to eat, and in Chapter 7 he builds a shelter and thinks of it as home: "Three days, no, two—or was it three? Yes, this was the third day and he had thought of the shelter as home" (72). Gail asked students to write journal entries on these topics after reading, and the results, again, showed students connecting to Brian's essential experiences as he begins his struggles to survive. Gail reported on how this writing about hunger enriched their discussion of Brian's situation at this point in the story.

> They talked about how Brian's primary focus throughout the chapter was on locating food. The students discussed his need for food as his basic need and his first instinct. Without food, he could not do anything. I was pleased when the discussion moved to the students' experiences with hunger. I asked them if they could remember a time when they were hungry. Many students mentioned situations in which they had not eaten for hours and were exerting energy. They discussed the feeling and lack of energy it created. These discussions again help the students to connect to Brian.

Gail also noted how one student boldly challenged in his writing whether hunger was the key theme of the chapter. As Gail writes, "The student said a better title/theme would be confidence. His reasoning: Brian worked hard and had confidence that he would find food. I was pleased with the student's willingness to deviate from the topic I suggested." This was significant because this student, at least, was analyzing the circumstances of the book for himself and interpreting its meaning, rather than simply completing another school task for the teacher. The book was becoming his own, not just a school assignment.

The discussion of "home" became a comparative analysis of Brian's shelter with how they imagined his home in New York and focused on what he didn't have in the woods. In the woods Brian—in Gail's phrase—"had to *earn* everything he had." And yet Brian in Chapter 7 does come to call his shelter a "home," and students examined how he created it to meet his needs and made it into a place for his survival. Brian was becoming acclimated to his surroundings.

Gail Barnhart and her class continued to explore Brian's survival as they made their way through *Hatchet.* They examined his self-pity in Chapter 8, discovering as Brian did that "feeling sorry for yourself didn't work" (82). They followed his attempts to make a fire, discussing why fire was important to Brian's survival.

Then, after working on *Hatchet* for nearly two weeks, a national event occurred that dovetailed perfectly with students' study of the novel: Hurricane Ike roared into the Texas coast. After laying waste to Galveston and flooding huge portions of Houston, Ike tore north into the country's heartland, then veered eastward, lacing much of Ohio—and the Crestview community—in terrible winds and rain. Power went out over most of Gail's school district, and her school was closed for two days.

When students returned to class, Gail used the incident to direct them back into *Hatchet.* What was it like, she asked her students, to be without power, and even without water (since many well pump systems were disabled in their rural community)? What must it be like for Brian, stranded in the wilderness with no comforts of civilization?

Gail followed this incident with another writing assignment in which students used sensory details to write first about their experiences during the windstorm, then, from Brian's point of view, about his struggles to survive. Whether it was because of their own connection to Hurricane Ike or because of their growing attachment to Brian, the class wrote vividly about Brian's situation.

Carter used sensory description to describe the plane crash.

> I heard the pilot yell in pain. Also I heard the plane rumble. I felt the
> rudder pedals under my feet. I felt the plane hit the trees and my head
> hit the side of the plane. My body ached with pain from the wreck. I

felt like giving up. I smelled the odor from the pilot when he had the heart attack. Your senses help you to survive in the wilderness.

Allison, too, vividly described what Brian was sensing as he found himself alone in the plane.

> I could see the plane soaring in the air through the sky. I looked at the dead pilot and was shocked. A smell of fear entered the room. I couldn't think over the sound of my pounding heart. I took a deep breath. I could feel the engine vibrate. The plane hit the water and I would smell dead fish and also a smell of pine. I felt the hot sand between my fingers. Finally the crash was over.

Finally, Matthew also put sensory description to use in re-creating how Brian perceived his situation in the woods.

> I feel the mosquitoes swarming my skin. I see them hovering over me like rain clouds. I hear the mosquitoes buzzing in my ears like a screeching whisper. I smell the juice of the berries as I fall asleep and hear the fire crackling like snapping twigs. I feel the heat surrounding me like a warm blanket. I smell the familiar smell of a smoky scent rising like the morning sun in the flames. I see the burning coals sending an orange flow of light hitting the walls like lava.

The class continued to read through the novel, sometimes individually as homework, sometimes with chapters read aloud, and they responded in dialogue journals about Brian's increasing resilience as he encountered one challenge after another. After several more chapters, Gail asked the students to pair together to write "I Am" poems focused on Brian and to illustrate them with representations of the survival theme. Gail reported,

> I was extremely impressed with the decorations, but more importantly, the poems were brilliant. The students really took the time to analyze Brian's thoughts, feelings, and desires. I was especially impressed to see that they focused on more than just survival. Many groups focused on his desire for his parents to reconcile and for the "secret" to be forgotten.

Several poems illustrate this accomplishment. Adrianna and Brooke collaborated on this effort:

> I am the best thing I have.
> I wonder when the searchers will come.
> I hear things I never heard before.
> I see the sunset on the lake.
> I want a good meal.
> I am the best thing I have.
>
> I pretend that my fire is alive.
> I feel the heat of the fire.
> I touch the handle of my hatchet.
> I worry that they will forget about me.
> I cry when I feel sorry for myself.
> I am the best thing I have.
>
> I understand my resources are low.
> I say that I need to get motivated.
> I dream about my parents and friends.
> I try to keep myself alive.
> I hope someone will find me.
> I am the best thing I have.

Benjamin and James wrote:

> I am determined and independent.
> I wonder if they will find me.
> I hear animal cries in the middle of the night.
> I see the deep blue lake and woods around me.
> I want to go home.
> I am determined and independent.
>
> I pretend I am a survival expert.
> I feel hopeless sometimes.
> I touch the holes in my calf from the porcupine.

I worry if I will be here forever.
I cry when I think they won't come.
I am determined and independent.

I understand I could be here forever.
I say to get motivated.
I dream I will be home eating a fresh meal.
I try to always have hope.
I hope they will find me.
I am determined and independent.

Drawings of hatchets, campfires, airplanes, bears, and juicy hamburgers appeared on these poems, alongside clip art and photographs of a porcupine, deep woods, and a glowing home in winter. Clearly, these students captured Brian's circumstances as he continued his struggles to survive.

When the class got to Chapter 13 of *Hatchet,* Gail asked students to describe the major changes in Brian after forty-two days in the wilderness. As he realizes at this point that he won't be rescued soon, if at all, Brian learns to adapt himself to his surroundings, and students cataloged those adaptations. "The new Brian listens, sees, and smells things differently," Gail noted in a summary of students' observations. "He is in tune with nature and aware that he is a visitor in the wilderness. He respects the animals. He knows not to step in between a mother bear and her cubs. He sees the wolf and nods to him, showing respect and appreciation. Brian understands that the wolf owns the area, and Brian is just a visitor."

A short while later, Gail had students create survival guides containing "eight tips on how to survive something they have lived through." Student guides included suggestions on surviving football, Mrs. Barnhart's class, divorce, younger siblings, a death in the family, and so on. Students followed this activity with written explanations of how to survive in the wilderness, based upon Brian's experiences in the novel.

One element of Brian's schooling about wilderness survival that Gary Paulsen emphasizes in *Hatchet* is Brian's ability to learn from his mistakes, and Gail had students note the missteps cataloged in Chapter 14, which begins with the word *mistakes* and repeats it over and over throughout the chapter. Students came to understand that survival is not based on avoiding mistakes, but on learning from them. They noted lessons Brian learned from encounters with various animals—that a bear won't attack unless her cubs are threatened; that porcupines and skunks can fight back despite their small size; and that a moose is powerful and territorial. One student noted that Brian's most important lesson overall was "Nothing in nature is lazy, so he [Brian] can't be lazy." Another noted of Brian's perseverance, "Even when you're just completely and utterly destroyed, you have to move on and live through life. That's just the way the world was meant to go." As Gail noted, these are "pretty impressive words of wisdom from twelve-year-olds."

As the novel drew to a close, students were asked to imagine what Brian's parents were thinking nearly two months after his disappearance. They wrote persuasive letters from the parents' points of view pleading that the search for Brian should continue. Matthew wrote to the rescue service as Brian's parents.

Dear Director,

I know that you are in charge of the search for my son, Brian Robeson. I also know that it has been most difficult trying to find my son, but I need you to keep looking. Every day I wake up and feel fine, but then the thought of Brian weighs me down like I'm stuck in the bottom of the sea. Brain's whole family is heartbroken about the crash and most of them think he is dead, but I know he is alive. I need you to keep looking even when all hope is lost.

Sincerely,
Karie and John Robeson

Finally, students assessed the "new" Brian at the end of the book by brainstorming once more a list of survival skills Brian had learned and by discussing the changes in Brian mentioned in the book's epilogue. Students brought this information together in new "I Am" poems about the book's protagonist at the end of the novel. Brooke captured the new Brian effectively in this verse of her poem:

> I am a new better person.
> I wonder if I'll go back to the forest.
> I hear the noise of the city.
> I see the city's lights.
> I want the peace of the forest.
> I am a new better person.

The Other Brian Books

Gary Paulsen had no additional plans for Brian Robeson upon completing *Hatchet*, but he explains what happened when the book became so successful.

> I wasn't going to do the sequel. But, I mean, we're talking 200 letters a day for five years or something like that, and that's a lot of mail. Thousands and thousands of young people wanted more about Brian. Brian had become alive to people, and I was holding back and wasn't going to do it, but then finally I got this call from the National Geographic Society, and they wanted me to tell them where Brian lives so they could interview him for the magazine. And I said, "You know, it's a novel."
>
> "Yeah, but he's a real kid," [they replied].
>
> They were absolutely convinced, and I said he wasn't real, and they said, "You changed his name, but he's a real kid." So then I decided that Brian had taken on a life of his own. (Salvner 1996, 45)

Because Brian had "taken on a life of his own," Gary Paulsen decided to write *The River* (1991), a sequel to *Hatchet*. In *The River*, Brian, now fifteen, is visited in his New York home by a survival psychologist, Derek Holtzer, and two military men, who are gathering information about survival techniques to teach at a military training school. After several interviews, Derek convinces Brian to take him back to the lake where he lived for fifty-four days to watch how Brian adapts to such difficult challenges. After the two travel to Canada and live for several days on the lakeshore, a storm comes up and Derek is struck by lightning. In a coma, Derek needs medical help, and so Brian builds a raft and floats him down a river to a trading post. Having learned how to survive by himself in *Hatchet*, Brian Robeson must now learn how to save someone else. *The River* extends Brian's character by teaching him new lessons.

Upon its publication in 1991, *The River* sold 346,000 copies within forty-three days (Salvner 1996, 45), convincing Paulsen that Brian had, indeed, taken on "a life of his own," and so in 1996 he published *Brian's Winter* (1996), an "alternative sequel" that takes Brian back to the end of *Hatchet* and presumes that the boy was not rescued by the bush pilot but must find ways to survive the bitter Canadian winter. As Paulsen notes in a preface to *Brian's Winter*, Brian's "previous knowledge was vital—he had to know summer survival to attempt living in winter" (2). And so, based on that summer knowledge, Brian adapts to the bitter cold of the north and learns new ways of hunting in winter and insulating his shelter.

In 1999, Paulsen released *Brian's Return*. As the novel opens, Brian has been having problems at school and home; he's unhappy with his life and feeling even more isolated than he had in the wilderness. As Paulsen writes, "He sought solitude. Even when he was in a group, nodding and smiling and talking, he was alone in his mind" (6).

After getting in a fight with a classmate, Brian begins to see a youth counselor. Caleb Lancaster is a retired police officer and is blind, and soon the boy's sessions with Caleb become reminiscences, in which Brian describes the wilderness he has been to so vividly that Caleb can picture it. After Brian suggests during a session that the only way he will understand his anger and his reactions to schoolmates is to go back to the woods, Caleb agrees and helps to arrange a trip back to Canada as summer begins. Back in the wilderness, Brian writes journal entries to Caleb and comes to feel "at home" once again. Meeting a trapper, Billy, at his campsite one day, Brian learns almost spiritual lessons about the world, lessons that finally diffuse his anger and leave him feeling settled. After Billy leaves, Brian has a dream about him, and after he awakes he realizes that "when he'd met Billy he was meeting himself years from now, an old man who looked carved in wood moving through and with the forest, being of and with the woods, and he decided that it wouldn't be so bad a thing to be" (109).

Although Brian has truly found himself at the end of *Brian's Return* and the original book jacket of that novel identified it as the "gripping conclusion" of Brian's story, Paulsen wrote still another Brian Robeson book afterward. Published in 2003, *Brian's Hunt* has Brian back in the woods once more, where he comes upon a half-wild dog who leads him eventually to the campsite of the Smallhorns, a Cree family that had befriended Brian in the wild. He finds the Smallhorn parents killed by a rampaging bear and their daughter Susan missing. With the help of his new dog companion, Brian tracks the bear until he finds her. Reassured that Susan is safe, he strikes out to hunt the killer bear as an act of revenge, but after killing the beast in a terrific battle, he looks upon the beast and understands a new lesson—that it was "not a villain, not an evil thing. Just a dead bear. Like any other dead animal that he might have hunted. Killing the bear did not bring back his friends, did not ease the pain for Susan and her brother and sister. It was just what it was, a dead bear" (98).

Animals are like all of us, Paulsen seems to be saying—hungry and looking for ways to survive. To see them as more or less is to misunderstand the world and our place in it.

Teaching the Other Brian Books

Gail Barnhart wanted to expand her students' experiences with *Hatchet* and its survival theme, and so she set up a literature circle approach to the other novels in the series. The idea of literature circles comes from Harvey Daniels, who proposed a group exploration of books in the classroom that would "turn traditional reading instruction upside down in almost every dimension" (Daniels 2002, 6) by giving students authority over what to read and what to do with the reading. According to Daniels, with literature circles the teacher's role shifts "from the presenter/questioner at the center of attention to an unobtrusive, quiet facilitator. In this classroom structure, the students are the ones making the choices, raising the questions, doing the talking, and making the meaning" (7).

Gail set up a modified version of Daniels' literature circles to serve her purposes in this unit on the Brian books. In a pure literature circle setting, students freely choose what to read and then organize into reading groups. In Gail's class, by contrast, this reading was limited to the four sequels to *Hatchet* written by Gary Paulsen. Her aim was to further explore the survival theme from *Hatchet* and to examine development of Brian Robeson's character throughout the series.

After completing *Hatchet*, Gail introduced the other Brian books to the class by book-talking them, reporting briefly on the key elements of each story. Then she had students state which titles they would prefer reading, collated their interests, and set up a group to work with each of the titles: *The River*, *Brian's Winter*, *Brian's Return*, and *Brian's Hunt*. Each student was given a copy of his selected work, and the groups began their reading.

Harvey Daniels proposes various roles for students to assume in their literature circles. Among them are Discussion Directors, who are responsible for setting up topics for discussion as the group reads. Connectors look for connections between the book and the outside world, and the Summarizer summarizes key events of the story as the group moves through it. A Literary Luminary selects favorite passages to read aloud during the discussions, and the Vocabulary Enricher notes unfamiliar words in the text (Daniels 2002, 77–94).

Gail gave these roles to students in her Brian Robeson literature circles, and they performed the tasks well. In serving as Discussion Director, for example, Matthew identified these topics as his group read *Brian's Winter*:

- How do you think Brian's flashbacks helped him in his survival?

- At the very end of the first half of the book, how do you think the snow will be an advantage and a disadvantage to Brian?

Cole served as Connector and observed to his *Brian's Winter* group that "Brian has to do things that he really doesn't want to do, like us." Adam, as Summarizer, gave an overview of the opening of *Brian's Return* by writing, "Brian can't get used to modern city life, so he decides to return back to the woods. Brian made a great friend named Caleb who is a counselor. He was forced to talk to a counselor after he beat up Carl, a football player."

Each group's Literary Luminary selected favorite passages to read aloud during the discussions, leading Benjamin to read these lines from the opening chapter of *Brian's Return*: "In that instant Brian totally reverted. He was no longer a boy walking into a pizza parlor. He was Brian in the woods, Brian with the moose, Brian being attacked" (9). As explanation for his choice, he noted, "I picked this passage because it informs the reader just how much being lost changed Brian." Alyssa served as the Vocabulary Enricher for the opening pages of *The River* and presented the words *phony, evasive, marooned,* and *marveled* to her group, while Michael identified *succulent, mukluk, anorak, implicitly,* and *scrutinized* from *Brian's Hunt.*

As the groups read their various Brian novels, they were also given both individual and group tasks to complete. Gail asked students, for example, to create survival posters on which they displayed a quote from Brian, several survival techniques from their book, and a rendering of one setting from the story, along with brief commentary on the importance of this place to the book. Students also were asked to write "villain" poems from Brian's point of view. These villains were not to be human but were to be situations or forces Brian struggled against. A whole-class brainstorming came up with the following possible villains to write about: winter, lightning, divorce, moose, and survival.

Adrianna began her villain poem about winter with the vivid line, "Winter is my Joker, always changing cards," and Adam wrote about divorce, using the lines, "Divorce is like a white T-shirt. Once it's stained it'll never come out" and "Divorce is a hungry piranha. It eats your life away."

At the end of the *Hatchet* sequels, students drew "beginning of book" and "end of book" illustrations of Brian and wrote descriptions of how he had changed. Adam captured Brian's changes in *Brian's Return* imaginatively by drawing the boy in prison garb at the beginning of the story to represent how life was a prison to him in the city and then drawing him fishing in a lake at the end, quiet and self-content.

As the literature circle discussions continued, Gail gave the groups a culminating project assignment: a Survival Museum. She set up the project with this note to students: "Your classmates are curious about your book and what happened to Brian in it. To lessen their curiosity, create a 'museum' to share what you learned about Brian from the book."

For the project, each group member was asked to select four items to display in the group's museum that focused in some way on the theme of survival in the story. Items could be artifacts from the novel or websites of information related to the book. During each day of Museum Week, a different group set up stations around the room that displayed these items, made use of computers linked to websites, and included posters explaining the displays.

The project was a huge success. *The River* group constructed displays on fire (showing flint and birch bark of the kind Brian used to start a fire), the river (containing a map of the river showing where Brian had to travel), and additional demonstrations about food, lightning, and a survival website. The *Brian's Winter* team prepared a trifold brochure about its exhibit, then had fellow students read a website article on winter survival and fill in a scavenger hunt worksheet. Museum "visitors" to this display also examined items in a survival kit the group assembled and matched pictures of animals Brian meets in the novel to descriptions of those creatures.

The students who read *Brian's Return* set up four stations around the room. In one, students were blindfolded to represent Caleb's blindness and asked to feel items Brian encountered in the wild. In another, students viewed a model of the book's setting. A third took students to a survival website to view information on wilderness survival, and the fourth displayed tools Brian used during his survival. The *Brian's Hunt* team displayed exhibits on fire safety, bears and tracking, hunting, and survival tools.

Asked what enables Brian Robeson to survive challenge after challenge in the Brian books, Gary Paulsen has said, "He *has* to survive; there are no safety nets for him in these books—no parents or teachers or friends or grocery stores or motels or guide books. If he's going to eat and find shelter, he has to do it for and by himself. There's nothing and no one except himself to rely on" (email correspondence 2008). Clearly, the students in Gail Barnhart's class learned this lesson that self-reliance is the key to survival while studying *Hatchet* and the other Brian books. As Jason noted in his before-and-after character comparison at the end of the unit, "Changing helps Brian survive throughout the two books I have read, and also changing helps everybody out during everyday life."

Gary Paulsen has been asked about his plans for the Brian books, in particular whether he intends to write more stories about Brian Robeson. Although no such books are in the works presently, Paulsen has been circumspect about whether he is finished with his famous character. "I have learned, I think, to never say never about my writing," he explains (email correspondence 2008). Readers of *Hatchet* and its sequels, including Gail Barnhart's seventh graders, can only hope that he is inspired to continue the story.

The Monument

Gary Paulsen in a Workshop Classroom

Margaret Silver is in her eighteenth year of teaching, the last three using a workshop design for her eighth-grade classes, modeled on the reading/writing workshop approach described by Nancie Atwell in books such as *In the Middle* (1988), *The Reading Zone* (2007), and *Lessons That Change Writers* (2002) and refined by suggestions in Harry Noden's *Image Grammar* (1999) and in Ralph Fletcher and JoAnn Portalupi's *Writing Workshop: The Essential Guide* (2001).

Meg's room at Southside Middle School in Columbiana, Ohio, is set up workshop style, with student desks pushed together in "pods" to enhance interaction and collaboration. Class time is spent on reading, drafting, responding, revising, and filing status reports about work completed and in progress. The focus is on students practicing the crafts of writing and reading, not on teacher talk about writing and reading.

Though students in a typical reading workshop choose their own works to read, at their own pace, Meg was interested in the idea of using a common book at the beginning of the year in order to establish some concepts of response and also to model positive reading habits. Gary Paulsen's *The Monument* (1991)—Meg's "favorite" Paulsen book—seemed to hold promise for this introductory eighth-grade experience.

About *The Monument*

The Monument is the story of Rachael Ellen "Rocky" Turner, a thirteen-year-old mulatto orphan who is lame and expects never to be adopted until Fred and Emma Hemesvedt from Bolton, Kansas, come to her orphanage and announce, "We want you to join our family and come to live with us" (10).

Fred and Emma are certainly not ideal parents. They both drink, but Rocky notes that "they have never, never done anything bad to me" (13), and she quickly settles into life in Bolton, where Fred runs the local grain elevator and Emma "sits at home with a big gallon jug of red wine and watches the soaps" (13). Rocky, along with her pet dog Python, acclimates to the slow farm life of the town.

Things change suddenly in Bolton when the town decides it wants to build a monument to its war dead on the courthouse lawn, and an itinerant artist named Mick Strum accepts the commission to design the monument and comes to town. Mick has the eyes and heart of an artist, and immediately upon arrival, he passes through the community, drawing whatever he sees. Rocky has never seen anything like him, nor has she ever perceived what art can be and do, and after following him around for a few days, she announces that she wants to be an artist herself, to which Mick replies, "You already are that—I knew you had the hot worm in you when I first saw you walking up to the station wagon" (83).

As Mick researches ideas for Bolton's monument, he teaches Rocky "something of technique, of line, of color—of art" (84), taking her around town and telling her to sketch what she sees, then giving her a book of Degas prints, which move her powerfully. After several days, Mick gathers the townspeople at the courthouse, where he has hung dozens of sketches of Bolton scenes and people. Some of the pictures are inflammatory, such as the nude drawing of Mrs. Langdon and the picture of Mrs. Carlson gripping a dollar bill with a greedy look on her face. The town's residents "explode" (to use Mick's term), showing their anger at this outsider who seems to be intruding on their lives, and Mick uses the reaction to get citizens talking about what art can be and does, and thus what they want their monument to be. After hours of discussion, the town slowly comes to understand what Mick already knows about them and about their best purposes for a memorial, after which he plans and constructs a simple row of trees on the courthouse lawn as Bolton's monument, each tree representing a fallen veteran from the town.

"Watch and learn and work and live and be" (104), Mick advises Rocky as she searches to understand art and herself. At the end of the book, after Mick Strum has left Bolton, Rocky writes him to report how the town—and she—have changed. She signs the letter *Rachael*, using her real name for the first time instead of the nickname representing her tough persona.

In an endnote to the novel, Gary Paulsen quotes Katherine Anne Porter about the durability of art ("Art is what we find when the ruins are cleared away") and then expresses his desire to show in the novel how art "can shake and crumble thinking; how it can bring joy and sadness at the same time . . . ," and "and how the beauty of it . . . can grow from even that ultimate ruin of all ruins, the filth of war" (151). Clearly, it is these shaping forces of art and war, beauty and destruction, which drive the novel forward.

Teaching *The Monument*

The shaping force of art is also what determined Meg Silver's motives for opening her workshop with this novel. In her journal, she noted that in *The Monument*, Paulsen

illustrates, much better than I ever will, the complications, the indi-
vidualities, and particularities of art. The novel, I hope, will give cre-
dence to the radically individualized and quirky nature of Workshop
in the classroom, and perhaps help kids to see the necessity of practicing real reading and writing in the classroom, if only for the rea-
son of staying true to Art (with the capital *A* here). We'll see.

Meg outlined three "big ideas" about art and literature in using
The Monument to introduce her workshop: (1) an awareness of
what is "true" or "authentic" about art and about reading and writing, (2) the importance of audience to art and to writing both, and
(3) the necessity of being engaged personally and honestly in acts
of creation—expressing the self one emerges from. With these in
mind, as the school year began, Meg Silver introduced her eighth
graders simultaneously to the new experience of a class workshop
design and to *The Monument*.

Meg chose to complete most of the novel as a read-aloud,
interspersing chapters in between training and practice in read-
ing/writing workshop, including self-selected reading and writing
experiences. As the class proceeded, she gave students extensive
opportunities for response to the novel through class conversa-
tions and in various writing tasks. Selections from these responses
illuminate the value of the novel for her purposes.

Gary Paulsen clearly is interested in the nature and role of art
in *The Monument*, and because Meg was interested to learn how
students perceived of art initially, she had them complete a prereading entry in their sketchbooks on the topic, "What is art?"

Some students perceived the topic generically, as one might
expect from eighth graders. Abby noted that art is "a way that people can express the way that they feel or how they see life," and
Elizabeth suggested that "art is something that can catch your
attention." As Meg noted in her journal, "Two students noticed the
'heart and soul' of imagination needed for art; one noted that art is
something 'amazing'; a fourth noted that art was something 'deep
down,' waiting to get out; and a fifth noticed that art was 'beyond
average' because of the feelings explored."

Even in these early speculations, however, some students began wrestling seriously with this broad, abstract question. In her sketchbook entry, for example, Callie pondered meditatively on what art might be for her, answering the question "What is art?" with this thought:

> [Art is] a colorful, musical, sad, scary, funny, or creative way of expressing the way the arts sees something. It doesn't have to be perfect or polished. It makes you think, feel, taste, smell, and laugh. It can leave you in silence, or make you talk nonstop about it. It can be messy, simple, orange, square, or soft. It can be a Van Gogh painting or a kid's crayon drawing. It could be your cousin's apple pie or a whittled piece of wood.

Meg followed up her initial sketchbook assignment with a second brief writing task in response to *The Monument*'s postscript, including the Katherine Anne Porter quote. Then she spent several weeks reading the book aloud as daily portions of her workshop sessions, inviting students to ponder how Mick, Rocky, and the town of Bolton perceived art.

After the book was completed, students wrote "literary letters" to Meg as responses to the novel. These responses weren't shaped by particular questions about art or any other theme or topic in the novel, but what is interesting is how often enhanced conceptions about art entered into students' commentary.

Hayley wrote, "I have never really been interested much in art and writing, but I think the book made me understand it a little more. It made me realize how much art is used in our everyday lives, and that it is almost everywhere you look." Lily reflected on Katherine Anne Porter's quotation and remembered her initial response to it before reading the book, then realized that her understanding had expanded: "I remember you had us read the quote before we started the book then write a response to it, and I remember thinking how my ideas were so good. Paulsen blew my response out of the water."

Even Brianna, who noted in her postreading response that *The Monument* was "definitely not my favorite book," still understood clearly its thematic exploration of art. Referring to Porter's quote, Brianna wrote, "That was powerful and most definitely relates to reading/writing/artwork. When ruins are cleared away and you work to express feelings about something bad that has happened, you often get stunningly beautiful results."

After Mick Strum comes to Bolton and begins investigating and sketching the town, Rocky Turner becomes captivated by him and his craft, deciding after only one day that "I want to be an artist" (83). Both Mick and Fred, Rocky's adopted father, tell her, "And how could it be any other way?" (83), suggesting that she has the soul and heart of an artist and that they have seen it in her all along.

Rocky asks Mick to teach her to become an artist, and Mick explains that he can't because she already is one, but he does explain that "I can teach you something of technique, of line, of color—of art" (84), after which he enables her to see that an artist must work from her inner view of beauty, not the public's view of what the work is or should be. And so Mick gives Rocky a tablet and pencils and offers a simple imperative: "Draw" (88).

Reading/writing workshop has a similar impulse to make students into readers and writers who are driven by their own emerging awareness of what needs to be said or understood, and Meg Silver's classroom made use of Rocky Turner's desire to become an artist by compelling students simply to write, as she was compelled to draw.

After beginning the reading of *The Monument*, Meg asked students to reflect in their sketchbooks on the questions, "What is real writing?" and "What is real reading?" Student responses implied, at least, that they were moving beyond the usual school perceptions of reading and writing into more genuine conceptions of these activities. Leah speculated that "Real reading is the kind of reading that doesn't put you to sleep or bore you to death. It keeps you up when you're sleepy, better than six cups of coffee." Andrew wrote, "Real reading is reading that you want to read, not forced to. It's reading till five o'clock in the morning and passing out with a book in your hands. It's getting a book that's 500 pages long and reading it in two days." Abby said, "Real reading is when you can't put the book down because it just takes you away."

Similarly, students speculated about "real writing" in their sketchbooks. Connor wrote, "Real writing is something you're passionate about instead of your teacher telling you what to write about." Brianna suggested that real writing was "writing with a purpose," and Amelia distinguished real writing ("any writing that comes from the heart") from "fake" writing ("something that is assigned that has nothing to do with you, like the essay questions on a test").

Would students have developed the same awareness of "real" reading and writing simply through the workshop experience, without the added influence of reading *The Monument*? Perhaps, but there was evidence in some of the ways they talked about reading, writing, and art that *The Monument* influenced their perceptions.

In final student responses to the book, many saw the explosion at the courthouse—where Mick Strum displays dozens of sketches of the town, including unflattering ones—as a high point of the novel. Similarly, in visits to Meg's class, I was struck at how often students referred to this explosion moment and, similarly, to Paulsen's allusion to the "bleeding pictures of Elvis or Christ on black velvet" (86) that the people of the town would favor if the artist didn't intrude with his own vision.

Clearly, this incident is partly about audience, Meg's second big goal for her unit. Mick is aware of Bolton's temperament and so understands how they will react. In responding to the writing of the explosion scene, Paulsen has said, "I think all good art provokes explosions in one way or another" (email correspondence 2008).

An awareness of audience came through in some of the "real writing" and "real reading" responses of Meg's students. Callie wrote that real writing was "expressing the experiences of yourself and others. . . . It's thinking about what your audience needs to hear, not just wants"—startlingly familiar to Mick Strum's distinctions between what Bolton residents need to see in their monument and what they want to see. Similarly, after noting conventionally that real writing "has correct punctuation, capitalization, and spelling" and "has an introduction and closing state-ment," Daniel moved into wholly different territory in his response by suggesting that real writing needs to "come from the heart and . . . get to an audience. People need to hear others' opinions and stuff."

In her journal commentary about the "real reading" and "real writing" sketchbook assignments, Meg asked herself, "How does this relate to Paulsen?" then opined, "I believe in these reflections that students are musing about the same things that Rocky muses about in the book. I like that that I've set up a sort of parallel jour-ney for my students, and that they can come to personal and artis-tic realizations as they read along."

One feature of Gary Paulsen's writing often praised by critics is his style—the way of telling a story, not just what happens to whom. James B. Blasingame, for example, in his critical biography *Gary Paulsen* (2007) in the Teen Reads series published by Greenwood Press, notes his attention to sentence lengths and types, as well as his use of repetition for effect (43–45).

Meg also was concerned about style in developing craft in her young writers, and one technique she employed was derived from Harry Noden's "brush stroke" analysis in the book *Image Grammar* (1999). Noden begins his work with the following comparison.

> The writer is an artist, painting images of life with specific and iden-tifiable brush strokes, images as realistic as Wyeth and as abstract as Picasso. In the act of creation, the writer, like the artist, relies on fun-damental elements. . . . Similarly, writing is not constructed merely of experiences, information, characters or plots, but of fundamental artistic elements of grammar. (1)

Meg hoped that students would be able to stretch their aware-ness of writing style by analyzing brush strokes in the books they were reading, including *The Monument*, but as she noted in her journal, "I found, mostly, that students were not ready for this stretch." Still, some students were perceptive about elements of Gary Paulsen's style, and Meg's attempts gave evidence that the approach was one worth considering.

Meg asked students to post examples of Paulsen's brush strokes on sticky notes displayed on a large square of construction paper mounted on the wall (which she called a "favorite workshop tool"), and alongside it, Meg displayed a second poster of notes on brush strokes of other authors these students read for workshop.

On the Paulsen poster, Connor noted that in *The Monument*, "In the beginning of each chapter there are reflections," using as an example the opening line from Chapter 10: "It came to me that night that I should be an artist" (72). Seth noticed the "vivid words" that Paulsen uses "to paint a picture in your mind of what is happening in the book," and then offered the example, "You know, when Harrison was young he went to sparking in that car and used to shine it and shine it so the emblem just stood out, caught the light and stood out. Just like on that drawing. How could that be?" (70). Alexis realized that Paulsen "ends chapters with short, strong sentences" like the statement ending Chapter 4: "Hello, Python" (22).

It's worthwhile to note that these observations about stylistic brush strokes seemed to carry over into students' awareness of what other authors they read for workshop did in their books. Meg mounted a second large poster on the wall entitled, "Our Writers' Brush Strokes," and on the sheet Andrew noted the "time shift he does between almost every chapter" in a Christopher Paolini novel. Christopher noticed the "headings over some paragraphs" in Laurie Halse Anderson's *Speak* (1999) that "make me want to find out what the heading means." And Josh saw noticed how Gary Soto "uses Spanish words to emphasize the main character's personality." Katherine noticed that in *Uglies*, Scott Westerfeld "compares objects to weird things," as in the opening line of the novel: "The early summer sky was the color of cat vomit" (2005, 3). Clearly, these young readers and writers, using Paulsen's *The Monument* as a starting point, were beginning to perceive how writers use stylistic "brush strokes" to create distinctive effects.

In addition to making use of *The Monument* to set up important features of a workshop classroom structure and to illuminate—through a conception of "art"—what good writers strive to do, Meg Silver found Gary Paulsen's novel to be an effective casebook for exploring important literary elements such as character and plot. All teachers who introduce literature to young readers might notice the value of Paulsen's work for achieving the goal of informing students about how novels work.

One literary element explored by Meg through *The Monument* was character. In her workshop, of course, she was concerned with giving students practice in creating and developing vivid characters in their own writing, but the impact clearly reflected back on students' perceptions and appreciation of the novel itself.

Meg engaged students in two different activities to highlight character development. First, she asked students to consider how writers develop characters, using the list "How to Develop a Character" from Nancie Atwell's *Lessons That Change Writers* (2002). Meg asked students to notice characters in what they were reading, and each student was asked to choose a vivid character from Paulsen's novel that was skillfully drawn.

Even students' choice of characters suggests how carefully they noticed Paulsen's handling of character, for the choices tended to go far beyond main characters such as Rocky Turner and Mick Strum. Two students chose Rocky's dog Python to analyze. Two others became intrigued with Rocky's adoptive father Fred, and perhaps most surprisingly, one took note of Mr. Jenkins' aged dog Rex—a minor character if there ever were one—who makes Rocky "think of old—old dusty dead and *old*" (64).

Meg then asked students to rephrase a description of their chosen character, using Harry Noden's "appositive brush stroke" from *Image Grammar* (1999), in which a descriptive sentence is interrupted by an appositive "re-name" of the character (7–9). About Python, Keira wrote, "Python, the fun-loving, smart, yellow dog, is a part of Rocky's family." Andrew wrote, "Python, the little demon, is Rocky's best friend." Seth stated that "Fred, an insightful alcoholic, knows a lot more than he shows," and Brianna wrote, "Rex, the ancient watch dog, was slow."

Clearly, students had noticed key details about character development in *The Monument*, and their re-creations of important traits were evidence of that.

In another activity, Meg asked students to locate "character quirks" in an important character from Paulsen's novel. Here's how she described the activity:

> We looked up *quirk* in the dictionary and found the words *idiosyncrasy* and *peculiarity,* and students came to a common understanding. We discussed, generally, why writers would create quirks in the first place, and students were able to say that: characters are more memorable, they are more interesting to read about, and they make for interesting thoughts and feelings in the story.
>
> We then created a list, together on the overhead projector, of twenty character quirks about Mick. At number ten, we came up dry. I was able to reassure students that this was "normal" and that our memories are only so reliable, and that looking back was a great reader's strategy. We all looked back, and students put what they found on little slips of paper. I used those "looking back" papers to compile the rest of the list, which I shared with students the next day.

Below are the first ten items students came up with about Mick:

1. He "knows" the future (p. 75, Mick knew where to find the popsicle sticks; p. 129, Mick realized what would happen at the courthouse all the time).

2. He drinks *way* too much.

3. He lives in his car.

4. He drives a station wagon.

5. He doesn't care at *all* what others think.

6. He says "Just Mick" when people try to call him by his last name (p. 77).

7. He sleeps with his butt in the air.

8. He "turns up" in strange places (car, garbage).

9. He has a gap in his teeth from a bar fight.

10. He frequently has chalk dust on his clothes.

After students consulted their books and wrote additional quirks on slips of paper, Meg generated these additional ten items to describe Mick Strum:

11. He smells bad (like "dead skunk").

12. His hands "fly" as he draws.

13. He cares about teaching people (Rocky, the town).

14. He might be in love with Tru.

15. He is true to his craft.

16. He can see things that others do not see (Mr. Jennings' "young" dog, the cross made of popsicle sticks).

17. He is a storyteller (the peach story, the stories about artists).

18. He takes risks (the "words" to the people in Texas, the courthouse scene, the nude painting).

19. He has a sense of humor ("shoot me now," Elvis on velvet).

20. He's homeless . . . moves from town to town.

Meg described where she took the class next in her journal.

After our common list, students made their own list about a character that they have read in a book this school year (past books from this term were fair game here). Again, students came up dry after a certain time, and they realized how "many" twenty could be. I liked that students needed to stretch, and that they needed to look back. This class, however, was much more willing and quick to do the looking back than my others [who had not read *The Monument* and not participated in this class experiment], and required less deliberate individual guidance because we had done the task together with Mick.

Clearly, Meg's use of *The Monument* with this class enhanced students' awareness of characterization and how traits and actions are used to create vivid, engaging characters.

Meg's class also examined plot as one of their explorations of this novel. Plot came up, in particular, when the class got to Meg's reading of the explosion scene at the courthouse, when Mick displays his drawings and the townspeople react powerfully, and often angrily, to how he has depicted them. (Indeed, Meg noted that this scene became an important touch point for the class in discussing plot development, and *explosion* became their own literary term for an important climax in a story.)

Meg reported that she became moved in reading that scene aloud to the class, and the students noticed her reaction and pondered it. They were invited to write questions and initial reactions to the events in the courthouse, after which Meg engaged them in a discussion of what happened. She described the conversation this way:

> The first question came from a student who asked, apologetically, "Is Mick a perv, you know, painting a naked woman?" Of course, I thought to myself, I teach eighth grade. This question was bound to be first. But luckily, I didn't have to handle my own explosion in my classroom, as other students came to my rescue. They were quick to point out to this individual that: there was a "connection" between Mick and Tru; the drawing was "true" and beautiful; that Tru picked the picture back up. I did ask the question directly: "Was Mick's drawing pornography?" Students were quick to say that there was a difference between "art" and sexual images for sexuality's sake. They understood the difference in purpose, and discussed it very maturely, actually. No guffaws or nudges from a one of them (again, those eighth graders surprise you every day!).
>
> The question came back from another as she looked to what to research from the book. She wanted to know why artists drew nudes—"and not because I'm perverted, Ms. Silver," she was quick to add.

So the action in this pivotal scene in the book stayed with Meg's students, and they moved to those literary speculations about cause and effect in literary action and about how motive drives the story forward.

Paulsen's powerful resolution of the story—when Mick has created a simple monument of trees on the courthouse lawn representing Bolton's fallen soldiers and when the townspeople come to view the monument after he has already left town—created another opportunity for students to respond to how well-paced, dramatic actions—even small ones—create powerful effects in stories.

Meg admitted that this final scene was also an emotional one for her to read. Here is how she described the class on that day:

> As I read, particularly at the end of the book (post-"explosion" as many of the students noted), you could hear a pin drop in my class. Kids were quiet, attentive, and reading or listening with an intensity that I see with only the most powerful of poems. On the day that I finished the second to last chapter, I was going to put the very last chapter on hold for the next day in order to fit in some individual novel reading. Students begged, "There's only one chapter left. Can we finish the book?" I asked if they wanted to read it to themselves, but they insisted on a read-aloud. So I finished the end of the book. One student later observed that she loved how quiet the class was after the last words were read from the book. "Everyone was so quiet. We just sat there and thought," she said to me. "That really shows how powerful the book was, Ms. Silver." The question that broke the silence was from a boy, who asked, "Were you crying at the end of the book, Ms. Silver?" I admitted that I was. I've read this book to myself at least five times, but when I got to the scene where Rocky describes Mr. Takern in her letter to Mick, I choked over the words "He didn't talk or anything, just sat, and once in a while he would reach over and pet the side of the tree, the bark, and I couldn't watch it after a while, but after a long time I will be able to draw it. I guess that's what makes an artist, isn't it?" (148–49).
>
> I answered the question posed by this student as honestly as I could. I said, "Y'know, I just couldn't get that picture out of my head,

of this old man patting the tree. And I've read this book at least five times through. It's a sad picture, though, isn't it? Reading it aloud somehow made it more sad, I guess. I was also moved that Rocky felt so strongly that she had to capture that moment . . . that the picture was so important. And Paulsen captured that moment for *us*, don't you see? I'm grateful that Paulsen made me see that picture, even though it made me cry, maybe *because* Paulsen made me cry."

Students didn't say anything more about those observations, and the conversation went into more easily anticipated questions, like why did Rocky sign her name *Rachael*? The read-aloud process truly made the art experience and the lessons that I hoped to teach much more powerful and immediate. We had this common, shared experience of art, and it moved us together. I think that this dynamic is one of the reasons that I read most of the novel aloud to kids. In my initial plans, I hoped to alternate the book reading between read-aloud and individuals reading in class, but felt compelled, and was often asked, to read aloud most of the time.

Here Meg commented simultaneously about method and content—about the power of reading aloud "even for eighth graders"—and about the way in which a well-constructed scene in a story can provoke thought and feeling. In other words, one lesson of the experience for students was a heightened awareness of how novels are not a string of events spread out over days and weeks, but are instead crafted stories whose pace and movement are shaped to produce effects, both cognitive and emotional.

Sketchbook responses to the explosion scene also validated that students understood and appreciated this dramatic high point in the story. Daniel wrote, "When the explosion occurred, it reminded me of my brother and me arguing about something. When Mick was talking about the explosion, I didn't know what he meant. But when it happened, it was cool." Andrew noted that the rising and falling action of the scene was "sort of like a roller-coaster." And Seth wrote, "I liked how Gary Paulsen described how they crumpled up the pictures that they didn't like. I could almost see this mob of angry people come and rip down a whole bunch of the drawings of themselves. I also really like how he described Harry's painting idea [his suggestion of a black velvet painting] 'of a soldier charging up a hill to save a blonde woman from avenging hordes' [133–34]. I think that it was ironic that it was on black velvet." This observation about plot structure and irony is pretty sophisticated for an eighth-grade student.

Asked about what he would hope that young people would gain from reading *The Monument*, Gary Paulsen said, "I don't think of what readers *should* take away when I write; I write because the story or the character interests me. That being said, having been an artist myself (I sculpted) and being a writer and loving music and reading the way that I do, I would say that I hope readers are aware of the 'art' that's all around them and that they feel they, too, in whatever way they choose, are artists and capable of creating something interesting and thoughtful and meaningful" (email correspondence 2008).

Meg's hope in using *The Monument* to set up her reading/writing workshop was undoubtedly similar—that students would learn how their own reading and writing, just like Mick's art, can be more than a school exercise, that they too are "capable of creating something interesting and thoughtful and meaningful." She affirmed this in a final class activity—a "gallery walk," in which students selected pieces of writing they were most proud of and posted them on the class walls for all to see and read. On the day of the gallery walk, these young people circulated throughout the room and wrote comments on sheets below each others' pieces of writing. Meg had reminded them to remain positive, and they did, commenting on a descriptive phrase here, a funny scene there, a poetic line that sang. There were no explosions during Meg Silver's gallery walk—only attentive, considerate readers and writers. Perhaps Paulsen's *The Monument* had helped establish both the tone and the positive result of this gallery experience.

The Crossing and Other Multicultural Books

Learning About Self and Others

Christa Welch teaches tenth-grade English at Sharon High School in Sharon, Pennsylvania, an old steel town on the Ohio border struggling to maintain economic viability and population. Christa's students are a mixed lot, both racially and socioeconomically, and they bring to her class a variety of academic talents.

Christa agreed to teach a unit for students on multicultural issues in Gary Paulsen's books, using *The Crossing* (1987) as the lead book, followed by small-group readings of three other works: *Sisters/Hermanas* (1993), *Dogsong* (1985), and *Nightjohn* (1993).

About *The Crossing*

In *The Crossing,* we meet two characters whose lives come to intersect in profound ways. Manny Bustos is a street urchin living in Juarez, Mexico, eking out a living day by day. Manny's mother abandoned him when he was very small, and while he has occasional memories of the nuns at the church where he was raised, his whole attention now is on survival. Manny begs for food from Maria, the woman who cooks tortillas at the Two-by-Four bar. He also begs for money from the *turistas* who cross the bridge between Juarez and El Paso and who, for entertainment, toss coins into the muddy riverbed of the Rio Grande below so that they can watch the children fight for them. Manny also picks up leftover food at the marketplace, and wherever he goes throughout Juarez, he is watchful for street men who abduct small boys for sale into the slave trade.

Minute by minute, day by day, Manny fears for his life, and he survives by holding onto the hope that one day he will be able to escape north across the river where, he has heard, living is more hopeful and stable and where he imagines he will be able to find work and build a life for himself.

Sergeant Robert Locke is stationed at Fort Bliss outside of El Paso, and on his nights off he makes his way to Juarez where he "would drink evenly and professionally until he was in a state that he called brain dead" (16). Robert Locke is "above all things, a sergeant" (13). He is "ramrod straight with graying, short, tight hair and a straight mouth . . . [and wears] a uniform so incredibly neat and sharp and true that the cloth looked to be carved from stone; a granite uniform" (14). When Robert Locke looks in the mirror in his small barracks room, he sees this "man in the mirror" looking back at him—this perfect, disciplined soldier.

But Locke has a second identity, and that is why he drinks. Sergeant Locke has lost comrades in war, and if he is not careful they find and haunt him with their cries of help. Locke cannot reconcile the fact that they have all died with the fact that he has not, and so, when not on duty, he drinks to suppress these hauntings.

Manny Bustos and Robert Locke come together in three chance meetings during *The Crossing,* and their relationship increases in complexity each time. First Manny attempts to steal from Locke while he is vomiting in the alley behind the Club Congo Tiki after a night of drinking. Despite his drunkenness, Locke grasps the boy's arm in a vise grip and won't let go, and the two make their way toward the bridge, where Locke intends to return to his base and where he finally releases the boy.

The second meeting comes near the marketplace where Manny has been begging food. He sees the sergeant walk into the Rio Brava Hotel and follows him, hoping to get some food. Sergeant Locke invites him to have breakfast, and the boy eats so much and so ravenously that Locke is reminded of a monkey he had seen while he was on leave in the Philippines—a monkey starved by its owners who then breaks free of his chain during an outdoor picnic and races across the table and starts "to grab and eat and grab and eat" (76). Manny convinces the Sergeant to attend a bullfight, but as Locke sees the bull stabbed and sinking to its death, he remembers his fallen friends, remarking to Manny, "All of this is to mean something and it's for nothing. Only a game. . . . I should not have come to this" (94–95).

A week later, Manny's life becoming even more desperate, the two meet again in the alley behind the Club Congo Tiki, where Manny decides to be totally honest with Locke by telling him of his desperation to survive, and he asks the man for help in escaping to the north. Locke remembers his comrades who also pleaded for help, but then—surprising even himself—he agrees to assist the boy. The book resolves quickly from there as the street men appear again and try to abduct Manny. Locke—transformed once more into "the man in the mirror"—brings the men down with blows while absorbing stabs from their knives. Sinking to his death, Robert Locke reaches for his wallet and gives it to Manny, stating, "Take it and run and cross and get the green card and live there. It is what you want. What I want you to have" (114). Holding the wallet, Manny runs to the river and his crossing.

 ## Teaching *The Crossing*

The Crossing is a masterful piece of writing, dark in tone and stunning in imagery, but it is not necessarily the most immediately compelling read for students. For one thing, short as it is at only

114 pages, the book's pace is measured and deliberate. Paulsen's trademark repetition of phrases and words slows the action even further. Second, the novel's third-person narrator keeps us at a distance from the main characters. There is surprisingly little dialogue in the book, and the action is reported in broken segments—character sketches followed by sections entitled "First Meeting," "Second Meeting," and "The Third Meeting and After." Finally, the experiences of Manny and Locke are significantly removed from most young readers. Most know little of the street life Manny endures in Juarez; nor do they necessarily have referents for Sergeant Locke's broken military persona.

In this context and with this awareness, Christa introduced the novel to her tenth graders. Christa identified two primary aims for the teaching of this novel. First, she set up instruction to highlight students' awareness of literary devices and elements present in the book in order to expand understanding of how a novel is constructed to create an impression on the reader. This was in keeping with general Pennsylvania standards for literature study at her grade level, and she documented these connections in her planning outline. Second, Christa wished to expand students' appreciation for the issues of multicultural identity and awareness as exploration of the book proceeded.

As the class began reading *The Crossing*, early discussions focused on characterization—understandably so as the novel's opening chapters are alternating portraits of Manny Bustos and Sergeant Robert Locke, the two primary "actors" in the book. As students were introduced to Manny, they voiced shock that he was only fourteen—younger even than they were. Though some Sharon High School students come from impoverished backgrounds, they still were startled by Manny's struggles to survive on the streets of Juarez, and they labored to imagine how someone so young could have already lived such a difficult, solitary life. Several were revolted by the references to the men who sought boys like Manny to sell into the sex trade.

There was also early speculation about a secondary character, Maria, who befriends Manny and occasionally gives him food as she cooks tortillas outside the Two-by-Four bar and café. Some thought that she might be related to Manny, others that she might have personal experience with crossings, which is why she cautions him against it. Although there is no evidence for either of these speculations in the novel, the predictions were evidence that students engaged with Paulsen's characters and developed an awareness of how literature is a combination of what the author provides us in terms of fact and inference and what readers bring to the text.

In other early days of the unit, the class engaged in lively discussions about *The Crossing*'s other main character, Sergeant Robert Locke. Initially, some students needed clarification about "the man in the mirror," thinking him to be a separate character rather than an element of Locke himself (evidence, perhaps, of the literal reading that many young adolescents still give to most texts). Once the character of Locke became clear to them, however, the conversation became rich. One student noted about him that "the man [Locke] people see is perfect [referring to the army poster here], but that's not who he really is."

Others compared these early portraits of Locke and Manny, engaging in that synthesis that we hope students will develop. They noted that both Manny and Locke were struggling and compared Manny's physical struggle with Locke's mental and emotional one. Both individuals, they noted, were preoccupied with crossing, but they were going in different directions. In a later discussion, one student, Dontrell, began to synthesize the two "faces" of Sergeant Locke by noting, "Locke gets drunk like he is on a mission."

Christa enhanced this synthesis by asking students to set up a three-column chart about the main characters in their notebooks. In the first column students jotted observations about Manny. Damian included factual details such as that the boy was homeless and was "skin and bones," but he also made analytical observations such as, "He is living his life as a lie." Khianna also recorded that Manny lived a "life full of lies," but added that he "told the truth at the end." Kanesha recalled that Manny "wants to be a man," and recalled physical features such as his red hair, large brown eyes, and long eyelashes.

In the last column of the chart, students wrote similar notes about Sergeant Robert Locke. Jack saw Locke as "the perfect soldier" who was "fearless" and yet "had trouble with memories of friends." Colin remembered the Sergeant as a drunk who "doesn't like pointless killing" and who finally "wants to help Manny."

Christa had students label a third column of the chart—the one in the middle—as "Same," and here students were asked to explore comparisons between the two main characters. It was in this column that some of the most perceptive observations about Manny and Locke appeared. Damian observed that "they both did not expect to find a friend," and yet "they both found a friend at the end of the story." Colin wrote that both characters were "lonely" and "struggling," but even more perceptively, that they both "see themselves as who they want to be." Kanesha observed that Manny and Locke "found friendship with one another," and Jack expanded that by including that they "didn't expect to become friends."

Discussions of these characters, and of additional minor characters such as the "coyotes" who take people north for money and the men who attempt to catch and sell Manny into slavery, continued throughout the unit, and insights were rich and frequent enough to suggest that Paulsen's characters had become "real" to the class and that students were expanding their awareness of how authors develop rich and engaging characters.

The Crossing also contains vivid settings, and students were captured by them as well. Certainly the streets of Juarez are sharply drawn, and throughout the story students commented on the danger and despair of that place for Manny. But they also had more precise observations about specific locales, including the Club Congo Tiki, where Locke goes to drink; the Hotel Rio Brava, where Manny begs a meal off Locke; and the bullring, where the two witness a bullfight and Locke notes that the fight was "to mean something," but that it's "only a game" (93–94).

What these settings have in common is their starkness, and that makes them vivid for students. The Club Congo Tiki is remembered for its garish entryway—the head of a native through whose open mouth customers walk, alongside painted palm trees until, once inside, they are greeted with equally garish and suggestive photos of two nearly nude dancers. The Hotel Rio Brava is a shabby place, "a no-nonsense hotel, old and full of dust and people" (69), and the bullring is a dirty stone arena in which grotesque rituals of killing occur.

Interestingly and not surprisingly, students' comments about these settings during class discussions and on a brief writing task Christa had them do on settings seemed frequently to run alongside their observations about one of the book's themes: truth versus lies, and in particular, Manny's need to lie to survive. Students clearly understood the "fakeness" of these places, enabling them to put analyses of setting alongside other thematic patterns in the book. Angelina noted at one point, "The club [Congo Tiki] is like a dream; Locke can lose himself and hide from the memories" there. Marisha observed, "Manny and the alleys and roads of Juarez are connected, the same." Clearly, students were using *The Crossing* to enhance their awareness of how vivid settings are put to use in an effectively written novel.

Observations about other literary elements surfaced during the class' discussion of *The Crossing*. Already in the first chapter of the book, Christa noted to students how Manny's hunger is personified, especially in the line, "It was almost a friend, the hunger, if something could be a friend and be hated at the same time . . ." (5), which Ayana explicated by noting, "The hunger is always there and it is comforting because Manny's life is so unsteady."

Symbolism—always a difficult concept for young readers—was touched on during the book discussions. Although they weren't necessarily introduced as symbols, the representations of Locke as "the man in the mirror" and Manny as the "pet monkey" that Locke remembers from his trip to the Philippines certainly included a symbolic awareness in the sense that each was a rendering of part of his corresponding character. The bull clearly was understood by students symbolically, and students several times made the connection between the loss of Locke's friends in war and the killing of the bull in the bullfight that he and Manny watch. When Locke notes that the killing of the bull is "for nothing" and "only a game" (94), Ayana observed, "I think he is saying that his friends died for nothing—that war is a game."

Another valuable literary element to explore in *The Crossing* is point of view. Interestingly, there are two main characters to the story, and the only credible way to keep them in balance is to use a third-person narrator who can comment on (and get inside) both of them. Christa asked students about the story's point of view, and they seemed to understand the necessity of Paulsen's choice of third person. Victoria noted that the story "would be very different [with a different point of view] because if it wasn't written in the third person, then we wouldn't know what the other person thought or felt." Megan commented on the necessity of the omniscient narrator, suggesting that without this device "we would not know what Robert or Manny are talking about because we wouldn't be able to know their thoughts."

Asked about the dual point of view of the story, Paulsen has noted its significance by suggesting that the book wasn't intended to be a single story, but two stories of his main characters: "It wasn't *a* story, it was *their* stories, so both characters needed points of view and it was important for me to have both voices in the novel because I felt like, at different times in my life, I had been like both Manny and Locke" (email correspondence 2008). Clearly, Christa's examination of point of view produced insight consistent with Paulsen's aims for the book.

A final extensive discussion of a literary element in *The Crossing* focused on plot structure, and this occurred most specifically as the students finished reading the book. In short, many didn't like the ending, during which, just as Locke promises to help Manny, the two are confronted by the men looking to sell Manny into slavery and Locke first kills their attackers and then dies of his wounds.

In class, one individual said, "I expected them to cross together," a perception that many other students voiced in their journals. Angelina wrote, "My reaction to this novel was that I think that the book was really good and that I wish that it was a little longer at the end because I wanted to know what happened to Manny after Locke died." Jack wrote, "I did not see the ending coming at all," and Colin was even more blunt, stating, "I really hate how they killed off Sergeant Locke. I also hate how they didn't tell us about what happened to Manny after he got Sergeant Locke's money. They didn't tell us whether Manny survived getting across or not."

The class discussed the book's ending at length, at one point reaffirming the conventional plot structure for stories that they had learned and knew: exposition, rising action, climax, falling action, resolution. The students came to realize that Paulsen had manipulated that structure in *The Crossing* by, essentially, chopping off the book's falling action and resolution. The class came to call this type of ending a "cliff-hanger," and references to it appeared in both the class' review for a final test on the book and in class discussions and journal entries.

What seems to have become clear to the class was that students had developed, over their reading careers, an expectation of "how a book works," which led them to expect that Manny's story would resolve more clearly at the end. Colin ended a final review of *The Crossing* by concluding, "Overall it was a good book, but I hope there's a sequel." Invited at the end of the book to imagine what happens to Manny after the novel ends, most proposed a resolution to the story in which Manny crosses into the United States and, after struggle, finds a way to survive. Victoria, for example, wrote a vivid ending in which Manny took Locke's wallet, sneaked to the river, crossed into the United States, and "got what he wanted and started living the American dream." Interestingly, however, a few responded as they imagined that Gary Paulsen would respond. Brianna, for example, wrote, "I think that Manny ends up getting caught and either killed or 'sold' just because Locke died and we didn't expect that."

Asked about his ending for *The Crossing*, Gary Paulsen has noted, "This was the right ending to the story because a pat solution would have been dishonest and insincere. Life is messy and doesn't always come with beginning, middle, end, lesson learned. And I think it's less important what I suspect happens to Manny than what each reader guesses or hopes or predicts" (email correspondence 2008).

It is clear from the discussion and class notes that students left their reading of *The Crossing* with an enhanced awareness of plot structure and of what happens when an author defies conventional patterns to create a particular effect.

In addition to expanding students' awareness of literary elements and how novels work, Christa had as a second teaching goal the development of "multicultural lessons"—an appreciation for how we are alike and different from one another. Literature is an excellent venue for the development of multicultural awareness. As Jean E. Brown and Elaine C. Stephens note in *Teaching Young Adult Literature: Sharing the Connections* (1995), young adult literature "has the potential to integrate and to unify learning in all content areas by celebrating the uniqueness of different cultures and their people while reaffirming the universal traits that define our humanity" (4–5).

This broad view of multiculturalism—that it is not so much specifically about explorations of race and culture, but instead about what unites and what distinguishes us as individuals and groups—lent itself well to what Christa was trying to accomplish in teaching *The Crossing* and in following the novel with several other Paulsen works that focus on identity and cultural difference.

One of the most vivid contexts for exploring these issues while reading the book came early on, as students came to understand Manny's desperate desire to cross into the United States. As Christa reported in her reflections on the unit,

> Many of the students saw several connections with *The Crossing* and the current border issues hitting the United States. We had a frank debate one day about the pros and cons of limiting immigration in the United States. Those students who were well versed in the issues shed light on the situation for those who perhaps pay less attention to the nightly news or who don't have parents at home who engage

them in such discussions. Students brought up several Sharon High School students who are of Mexican ancestry and questioned why their families should not have been allowed entry into the United States. It seemed that when names were put to the situation, closed minds opened a bit. We talked a great deal about the freedoms citizens are allowed within the United States, and we discussed how perceptions shape policy.

Manny's experience also seemed to put a "name to the situation" for students, and in discussions they clearly sympathized with his struggle to survive. Concern was voiced early and often about Manny's poverty, lack of safety, hunger, and struggles to survive on the streets. When discussion came to the early scene in which Manny tries to catch money thrown from the bridge by tourists and soldiers, the students reacted strongly. Several made the observation that the act of throwing money was "cruel, depressing, degrading, and ignorant," and the discussion extended to the observation that Americans are that way because they have money to throw away. One student personalized the observation, reflecting, "If I'm at a store and my change is fifteen cents, I tell them to keep it." Students seemed amazed that Manny was beaten by Pacho, one of the other boys, for only a dollar.

When the class came to the incident of soldiers spitting from the bridge onto the begging children, the discussion became even more animated. One student noted that "Soldiers spit because they are racist toward Mexicans," to which another observed, "Maybe things like that are part of why we get a bad reputation." A third reflected, "I saw kids begging like that when we were on vacation," and the class seemed to be wholly engaged in these matters of class and race at this point in the book.

It happened that the group's work on *The Crossing* paused on September 11, when Christa read the picture book *The Man Who Walked Between the Towers* (Gerstein 2003) to the class to reflect on the anniversary of the terrorist attacks on the World Trade Center in New York. Mordicai Gerstein's book tells the story of Philippe Petit's daring tightrope walk between the two World Trade Center towers in August 1974. Petit is a street performer, determined to accomplish this stunning feat, and he and friends manage to stretch a cable, onto which he steps into the air between the towers. As policemen attempt to bring him down, Petit moves to one side, then the other to remain on the wire. As Gerstein notes at one point, "As long as he stayed on the wire he was free" (30). The ending frames of the picture book make clear that this story is, in part, a patriotic memorial to the towers, the memory of which remains even after the terrorist attacks of 2001.

What is interesting about students' reactions, however, is that they made associations between the work and their reading of *The Crossing*. In particular, students saw similarities between Manny and Philippe. Comments included "Both are looking for freedom," and "Both will do anything to fulfill their dreams." It seemed as if *The Man Who Walked Between the Towers* enhanced students' reading of *The Crossing*, and vice versa.

About *Sisters/Hermanas, Nightjohn,* and *Dogsong*

Christa planned to follow her whole-class reading of *The Crossing* by literature circle explorations of three other Gary Paulsen books that resonate with that novel: *Sisters/Hermanas* (1993), *Nightjohn* (1993), and *Dogsong* (1985). All three coincided with her goals for the unit by addressing the same multicultural themes found in *The Crossing* and by enhancing students' awareness of literary devices and elements.

Sisters/Hermanas is a brief novella about two fourteen-year-olds, Traci and Rosa, who live in the same Texas city but come from wholly different backgrounds. Rosa is an illegal immigrant from Mexico City who imagines herself becoming a famous model but who actually survives by selling herself on the streets. Rosa has escaped north to find work, and she sends a portion of what she earns back home to her mother. The rest she spends on food and a shabby room at the Prairie Deluxe Motor Hotel, as well as on the garish, revealing clothes of her trade.

Traci, by contrast, lives in a large home in the suburbs, and as the novel opens, she is obsessed with trying out for the cheerleading team at her high school. Traci has everything she wants, and she is driven to believe that "nothing was ever bad, nothing was ever impossible, nothing was ever ugly, nothing was ever, truly, wrong" (21) by her mother, who is obviously living vicariously through her daughter's beauty and ambition to find a "perfect" life. "You can be anything," Traci's mother exhorts her, "but you must work on your looks" (23).

Sisters/Hermanas is written in alternating vignettes focusing on the two girls, in much the same way that *The Crossing* alternates portraits of Manny Bustos and Sergeant Locke to advance the story. Back and forth we go from the streetwalking Rosa (who dreams of fame) to the cheerleading Traci (who trusts her mother that her own fame will come through looks and personality). As Rosa prepares for work, Traci prepares for tryouts. As Traci's mother drives her to school in her Mercedes, Rosa makes her way through the shabby streets on her way to meet her "regular" customers.

The climax of *Sisters/Hermanas* comes when Rosa dodges from her usual route to avoid a watchful policeman, and she ends up at the suburban shopping mall at the very time that Traci's mother has brought her there to celebrate her successful tryout. Looking through a rack of dresses at a fashionable clothing store, Traci comes upon Rosa hiding between the dresses, just as the security officer approaches.

"We are the same" (64) is Traci's first impression as she sees the frightened Rosa look up at her. As Rosa is apprehended, Traci's mother strongly rejects that response from her daughter, exclaiming, "No. No, you aren't. She is what . . . she is what you might have been, could be, if you weren't like you are now" (66), meaning that Traci would be equally desperate if she were not popular, not the best. As Rosa is taken into custody, Traci's mother turns Traci back to the dresses: "Now, was it the red one you wanted?" (66).

Sisters/Hermanas is simultaneously printed in English and Spanish, back to back, a format that captures the cross-cultural implications of the book. In much the same way that *The Crossing* blends Manny's Mexican heritage with Sergeant Locke's military background, *Sisters/Hermanas* intersperses the points of view of two teen girls who, on the surface, are wholly different, but inside are not. Traci is correct when she observes, "We are the same" (64). *The Crossing* and *Sisters/Hermanas* make excellent companions in the classroom.

Gary Paulsen wrote *Nightjohn* after years of reading slave journals. Originally interested in writing a young adult biography of Thomas Jefferson's slave and mistress Sally Hemings (to whose memory *Nightjohn* is dedicated), Paulsen became fascinated by accounts of slaves who risked their own survival to teach slave children to read and write. *Nightjohn* is actually based on several slaves he read about, and the book pays homage to these individuals and others like them (Salvner 1996, 89).

Nightjohn is narrated by Sarny, a twelve-year-old slave at Clel Waller's plantation. One day John is brought in "bad" (naked and dragged by a rope) after Waller purchases him, and soon he begins to teach Sarny how to write the alphabet. Carelessly, Sarny sketches words in the dirt, and Waller catches him. First Sarny's wet nurse, Delie, and then John himself are whipped and punished for allowing this to happen. Waller notes that teaching slaves to read and write is against the law, and John, too, understands why this is so: "'Cause to know things, for us to know things, is bad for them. We get to wanting and when we get to wanting it's bad for them" (39).

The violence in this brief novel is jarring. John carries the scars of previous beatings on his back, and he and at least two others are whipped severely during the story. Trying to escape results in being hunted down and killed, and teaching slaves to read results in John's toes being severed. After this final assault, John does escape, but just as life gets back to normal for Sarny, he appears again and continues his lessons. John sets up a "pit school" deep in the brush so that Sarny and other children from nearby plantations can receive lessons each night. The novel ends with a rhythmic postscript entitled "Words," in which Sarny begins to tell the story of

Nightjohn, ending a cadenced series of statements with the asser-
tion, "Late he come walking and it be Nightjohn and he bringing
us the way to know" (92).

Paulsen's anger over slavery rages in the coarse scenes of
Nightjohn, and certainly his outrage shapes our awareness of a dark
period of American history, a time when humans were bought and
sold as commerce, when individuals were denied all rights and
opportunity on the basis of race. Any Paulsen unit on multicultural
difference and identity is certainly aided by a reading of this slim
but powerful work.

Gary Paulsen's Dogsong served as the third selection for the literature circles portion of Christa's unit. Dogsong is, in ways, unlike
Nightjohn and Sisters/Hermanas. It is longer than the other two
books combined, and it presents challenges to inexperienced readers, especially in the work's dream sequences.

Russel Suskit is fourteen, an Eskimo boy living in a small village on the Bering Sea. His mother has run off with a white trapper, his father drinks and prays to Jesus, and Russel seeks for some
fulfillment in his young life. "I am not happy with myself" (9), he
realizes, and he turns to the village shaman, Oogruk, because he
instinctively believes that learning his people's "old ways" will
somehow give his life focus and direction.

Oogruk owns the village's only dog team and sled, and though
he is aged and blind, he shows Russel how to use it. Slowly Russel
discovers the rhythms of his people's past as he takes runs out of
the village with the dogs and practices hunting with Oogruk's
ancient bow and spear. As Oogruk is about to die, he tells Russel,
"There is a thing you must do now to become a man. You must not
go home. . . . You must leave with the dogs. Run long and find
yourself" (72), and so Russel leaves on a long "dreamrun" north to
find himself and his destiny.

On the way, Russel dreams of an ancient Eskimo hunting a
wooly mammoth, and the two hunters' lives become intertwined.
Russel comes upon a pregnant girl who has left her village in
shame, leaves her to hunt food, and eventually returns to rescue
both her and himself. The novel ends with Russel's "Dogsong," a

song of his dogs, his people, Oogruk, and himself—a song of identity.

Teaching *Sisters/Hermanas, Nightjohn,* and *Dogsong*

Christa set up the second portion of her Gary Paulsen unit by organizing students into literature circles to explore these additional three Paulsen novels, in much the same way that Gail Barnhart set up her class to teach students about survival through Paulsen's Brian books. (See Chapter 2.) Separate groups of five or six students were created to explore each book, and students were taught some of the roles outlined by Harvey Daniels in *Literature Circles* (2002): Connector (finding personal connections to the work), Discussion Director (generating questions for discussion), Literary Luminary (selecting key quotes worth talking about), Vocabulary Enricher (vocabulary locator), and Illustrator (one who sketches key scenes or characters for review by all) (77–84). Each group worked through its selected title, rotating roles as it went along, and it was responsible for a final PowerPoint presentation to the class about its book.

These final PowerPoints verified that this added reading enhanced Christa's goals for the unit—expanding students' awareness of how literature "works" and establishing some unifying thoughts about how people are shaped by cultural identity. All groups seemed to develop an enhanced awareness of characterization in the novels. A group exploring *Dogsong* not only noted essential characteristics of Russel but also recorded that Oogruk's dogs were a mix of "wolf, Mackenzie River huskies, and Coppermine River village dogs." One group reading *Sisters/Hermanas* made deft and insightful comparisions between Rosa and Traci, noting Rosa's desire for fame based on her appearance (being on the cover of *Glamour* magazine, for example) and Traci's mother insisting that the girl "work now on what you will get later" (26) by focusing on her looks. Traci's careful preparation for cheerleader tryouts (taking three hours rather than the usual two) was paralleled with Rosa's preparation for her night of work as she cleans and puts on her leather skirt. "We are the same" (64), Traci notes, and the students skillfully showed how the two fourteen-year-olds were, indeed, the same.

As students worked on the group PowerPoints, they were also asked to complete a few individual tasks. In one they wrote journal entries from the point of view of major characters in the books— Rosa and Traci in *Sisters/Hermanas*, Russel in *Dogsong*, and Sarny and John in *Nightjohn*. Students' journal references to events from the novels revealed both their understanding of their characters and an awareness of how changes in point of view can alter a story. For example, one student insightfully imagined Rosa describing the climactic scene in the store at the end of the novel by observing how Traci's mother gave her "a dirty look like she is better than me." Another, writing as Traci, ended her journal entry, "Maybe Mom will one day not be so crazy about me always being the best or prettiest." The speculations about Traci's mother were clearly an extension of the actual story, and they revealed students getting "inside" characters and thinking from their points of view.

Symbolism also was explored by the literature circle groups. The group reading *Dogsong* noticed the symbolic nature of Russel's dream as it "guides him throughout his journey." The group reading *Nightjohn* astutely noticed symbolism in the novel, noticing how Clel Waller's whip symbolically represented his power and how the letters Sarny learned to scratch in the dirt represented freedom for her and her people.

Christa's report of the literature circles section of the unit expressed her initial disappointment that students didn't seem to focus on the cultural themes in the stories, but she noted that after the PowerPoint presentations, the links became clearer. She wrote,

> I think the students did pick up on the multicultural perspective, although they didn't identify it as such until we began to discuss the concept as a class. They began to see connections especially during the PowerPoint presentations, when each group was given insight into the other novels. They seemed to make sense of the well-

rounded perspectives to which they had been exposed. After the presentations, many students asked to sign out the other books, which I took to be a sign of success.

The cultural elements of each story were apparent in the PowerPoints—as a *Nightjohn* group, for example, centered on the Southern plantation setting of the book and the time of slavery that located it. A group examining *Sisters/Hermanas* focused not so much on the cultural differences between Rosa and Traci as the economic ones—Traci's family's beautiful suburban home contrasted with the decrepit Prairie Deluxe Motor Hotel where Rosa pays weekly rent. The *Dogsong* group tried to imagine how Russel's life was different from their own as they asked the question,

> Could you imagine living on your own at age fourteen, killing animals for food, sledding across the ice with nothing but five dogs to keep you company, a bow and a lance? Russel Susskit was hoping to find his own song by living by himself on the snowy tundra of the Arctic, risking his life every day to the cold, animals, and starvation.

Other Extensions

Christa's approaches to Gary Paulsen's multicultural novels not only offer rich opportunities for using these works in the classroom, but they also imply other extensions for productively engaging students in an expanded study of self and others. One possibility might be to expand Christa's use of the chart identifying qualities of Manny and Sergeant Locke in *The Crossing* and qualities that make them "the same" into a broader, whole-class chart that also lists qualities of characters from *Nightjohn*, *Sisters/Hermanas*, and *Dogsong*. The chart might be constructed with additional columns listing parallels in characters from different books. One column, for example, might invite the class to find similarities in Rosa from *Sisters/Hermanas* and Sarny from *Nightjohn*. Another might list qualities that make Russel from *Dogsong* like Manny from *The Crossing*. Perhaps adult characters from the novels might be compared in additional columns. Students, for instance, might find some interesting attitudinal parallels between Clel Waller in *Nightjohn* and Traci's mother in *Sisters/Hermanas*. A culminating activity in constructing such a chart might be to add columns at the end that identify "How We Are Different" and "How We Are Alike" in which the class constructs lists of ways in which the characters they have met in these books are like them or different. Any study of multiculturalism needs to become personal at some level, and placing Paulsen's characters alongside the students in our classes to discover similarities and differences might be a way of doing so.

Christa's PowerPoint project as a culmination of the literature circle exploration of *Nightjohn*, *Sisters/Hermanas*, and *Dogsong* might also, with a little imagination, be expanded to further dramatize the multicultural theme in the novels. Imagine setting up, for example, a classroom "cultural fair" in which groups not only project their PowerPoint about their novel, but also create displays of cultural artifacts that correspond to the books they've read, in much the same way that Gail Barnhart had her students construct a Survival Museum to display knowledge and artifacts from Paulsen's Brian books. It's easy to imagine students finding websites to display Inuit culture from *Dogsong*, Catholic religious icons similar to those Rosa kept in her room in *Sisters/Hermanas*, and bullfighting information consistent with the bullfight scene in *The Crossing*.

All four Paulsen novels examined in this chapter describe food from their cultures and times, and so students might try to cook (or at least display recipes for) the corn tortillas Maria cooks for Manny in *The Crossing*; the buttermilk, corn bread, and pork fat gruel that the slaves are served out of a trough in *Nightjohn*; and the seal and caribou meat Russel eats with the ulu, or the caribou eyes and muktuk (whale blubber) that Oogruk yearns for in *Dogsong*.

Customs in clothing, community life, and occupations depicted in the books might be displayed also in this cultural fair, as well as depictions of family patterns, economic circumstances, and ethnic customs. It is easy to imagine a classroom full of displays that, taken together, offer students cultural presentations that highlight similarities and differences among peoples and individuals—a perfect way to bring together a class' study of these novels.

Gary Paulsen has said of writing *The Crossing, Nightjohn, Sisters/Hermanas,* and *Dogsong,* "I don't write books because I hope to teach anyone anything. I wrote about those cultures because that was where the stories came from, not to make a point. I wasn't trying to capture a cultural identity . . . as much as I was trying to tell an individual person's story" (email correspondence 2008). At the same time, however, he has also said in regard to his interest in writing for young people, "We [adults] have been stupid. We have been lazy. We have done all the things we could to destroy ourselves. If there is any hope at all for the human race, it has to come from young people. Not from adults. We're too old. . . . We blew it" (Salvner 1996, 121).

Taken together, these two statements perhaps capture what Christa and all teachers might hope to accomplish by using these novels in the classroom. The idea is not to preach to students about what they should do or be, but rather to provide images of how life is, and by comparison, of how it might be. If young people are our hope, then an exploration of self and others needs to be part of our curriculum. Our future depends on awareness of, and appreciation for, what combines, and what distinguishes, us.

In her essay "Who Am I? Who Are You? Diversity and Identity in the Young Adult Novel," Lois T. Stover (2000) suggests three goals for using culturally diverse literature in the classroom:

> The point is that in our multicultural society and increasingly inter-connected world, we need to emphasize certain goals of the literature program. Through their reading, students should be able to (1) explore issues of self-identification and ethnicity, (2) explore the relationships between themselves and others, and (3) explore the relationships between and among cultures. The inclusion of YA novels about adolescents from diverse cultural backgrounds in the literature curriculum should help accomplish those goals. (102)

Clearly, Gary Paulsen's works are among the young adult novels that address these goals. Clearly, too, Christa Welch's use of *The Crossing*, *Nightjohn*, *Sisters/Hermanas*, and *Dogsong* in her tenth-grade class demonstrates how these goals might be addressed alongside other aims for literature study.

Other Patterns, Other Teaching

The body of Gary Paulsen's work is so large that it's relatively easy to find other patterns or qualities in them that invite classroom exploration. Certain character types, stylistic elements, and themes occur often, and they might be explored in the context of a single book, read by the whole class, or by a collection read as a unit or in literature circles. What follows are some other suggestions for using Gary Paulsen to accomplish various goals in literature teaching.

The Mentor as Character Type

Because young people are the protagonists of most of Paulsen's books, and because his stories follow the common pattern in young adult literature in which adolescents find their way toward greater maturity and adulthood, Paulsen is always looking for situations or people who might help these young people on the journey, and his primary helpers are of the classic character type of the mentor.

Paulsen's mentors are rarely parents (perhaps reflecting his own family life). Rather, they are older adults that these young protagonists meet along the way, and Gary Paulsen seems to take particular delight in making these mentors not superstars but flawed, yet decent, human beings. They take the form of artists (Mick Strum in *The Monument* [1991]), soldiers (Sergeant Locke in *The Crossing* [1987] and Waylon Jackson and Wayne Holtz in *The Car* [1994]), and relatives (Uncle David in *Popcorn Days and Buttermilk Nights* [1983]), but regardless of their identities in the stories, they are there to perform the roles of mentor and teacher.

As we have seen in Chapter 3 of this book, Mick Strum comes to rural Bolton, Kansas, to design a monument for the town, but his task becomes extended when he takes stock of what, and who, he's dealing with. Early on he meets young Rachael Ellen (Rocky) Turner, and he becomes her mentor, teaching her about art (giving her a book of Degas' works, for example); about how to honor life and loss (showing her what a monument to soldiers needs to be); and about herself (teaching how to accept and value who she is and what she is capable of). "Watch and learn and work and live and be" (104), Mick counsels Rocky, who does just that and comes to greater acceptance and understanding through his guidance.

Sergeant Robert Locke of *The Crossing* (discussed in Chapter 4) is another classic mentor who struggles with his own imperfections and flaws but still manages to offer the street urchin Manny Bustos protection and, finally, a chance at escape and a new life. Uncle David in *Popcorn Days and Buttermilk Nights* provides the magic of a carnival to protagonist Carly and the other children in his rural Minnesota town, and at the same time he offers the boy constancy and a model for how to live. Guided by Uncle David's model of hard work and consideration for others, Carly eventually begins to notice a change in himself.

> There was a whole new feeling in me—not just a change but a whole new thing. I didn't think everybody was against me any-more—I didn't feel that the whole world had been designed just to dump garbage on my head, which I had come to believe for a time in

the city. I was still fourteen, still caught in the same world, but there was something else now. I was . . . settled, somehow. (69)

There's another pattern to Paulsen's mentor characters, and it invites rich classroom discussion and analysis. Virtually all of the author's teachers or mentors are flawed characters who rise above their limitations to provide help and guidance to young people. The most common fallibility for these characters is the alcoholism that emerges out of Paulsen's own experience. Mick, Sergeant Locke, and Waylon Jackson from *The Car* all are consumed with drinking during their stories, the latter two of whom apparently drink to forget the ravages of war that they have witnessed. This "flawed mentor" character invites all kinds of valuable classroom discussion. Students might explore where bravery and compassion come from, for example, or examine Paulsen's human but still heroic mentors alongside the false "superhero" characters of today's popular culture. They might analyze the choices that a mentor makes to salvage a life of difficult circumstances, or the lessons that a hard life might offer.

Gary Paulsen also has given us some strong women mentors. One is the grandmother Alida in the autobiographical stories *The Cookcamp* (1991), *Alida's Song* (1999), and *The Quilt* (2004), who shelters the young protagonist in the stories and guides him with love and reassurance. (The grandmother is based upon Paulsen's own grandmother, Alida Moen, who gave the young Gary Paulsen the same guidance and love as the character in the novels.)

Another female mentor is Miss Laura in *Sarny* (1997), whom Sarny works for in New Orleans. Miss Laura is a wealthy and shrewd businesswoman, and she supports Sarny and eventually leaves most of her estate to her. But Miss Laura's legacy is not so much in what she gives to Sarny as in what she enables the young former slave to do. It is Laura who reminds Sarny that she was born to make a difference in life, and it is Laura who encourages Sarny to become a teacher to her people.

Imagine the benefits of clustering a teaching unit around these many teacher/mentors. Typically we instruct students in character development and character type by asking them to record details of a single character in a single book, hoping that they'll then extract understanding about how authors shape and use characters that can be transferred to other books. With a Paulsen unit on the mentor/teacher character type, students might be invited, as a whole class, to record character qualities from many books and then assemble a character profile of this type of individual. Equipped with such a profile, students might be asked to watch for other mentors they meet in their reading throughout the year, laying those characters alongside the portrait they've already drawn from Paulsen's works. (A playful way to do this might be to ask students to play a "Where's Waldo?" kind of game in their reading, based upon the hugely popular picture book series. From book to book, students might be trained to look for mentor characters hidden in the folds of a plot or setting. Mentors/teachers are so common in books for young readers that it shouldn't be surprising to have students come into class after further reading of a novel or story with the exclamation, "Found one!")

Teaching Style with Gary Paulsen

Style—the way a story is told—is one of the most elusive literary elements to teach young readers, who often are so fixed on the dramatic elements of a story—especially plot and character—that they don't even notice what the author is up to in the way sentences are framed and words are chosen.

And yet style is a worthy subject for instruction. Students who become acclimated to stylistic elements become more appreciative of what a good writer does (and thus become also more observant of what some poorly written stories don't provide). Many famous writers—and many who write for young adults—have counseled that to become a good writer, one needs also to be an attentive reader, and certainly some of what they have in mind is that one who reads observantly discovers what writers do, and thus what they might do in their own writings.

Gary Paulsen is a master stylist, but his writing is neither complex nor inaccessible, and so he's a perfect teacher of style. When reading Paulsen's works, one feature students might be invited to notice is repetition. (Indeed, repetition was examined by Gail Barnhart and her students, as discussed in Chapter 2.) Repetition is particularly visible as a device for creating suspense in works like *Hatchet* (1987), which contains numerous passages of repetition like this one, in which Brian Robeson is captured by fear as the engine of the plane coughs out and he realizes he is about to crash.

> He was stopped. Inside he was stopped. He could not think past what he saw, what he felt. All was stopped. The very core of him, the very center of Brian Robeson was stopped and stricken with a white-flash of horror, a terror so intense that his breathing, his thinking, and nearly his heart had stopped. Stopped. (12)

Repetition is also used in Paulsen novels to create a storytelling quality. Notice the repetition of the refrain "And it was true" in this story about a woodcutter told by Uncle David in *The Winter Room* (1989):

> They said many things of him. They said he could put a match in a stump so the head was sticking up and swing the ax with his eyes closed and catch the match perfectly so that it would split and both sides would light.
>
> And it was true.
>
> They said he shaved each day with an ax and never cut himself and his cheek was as smooth as a baby's.
>
> And it was true.
>
> They said he could take a four-foot piece of cordwood and swing two axes, one in each hand, swing them into the two ends and the wood would split clean and the axes would meet in the middle.
>
> And it was true. . . . (90–91)

Students might use passages like these as models and then write their own descriptions of an event that triggers a strong feeling, using repetition to create the effect, or write a story in which the storyteller creates emphasis and rhythm through the use of a refrain.

Another common stylistic feature in Gary Paulsen's writing is the use of metaphors and similes, and it can be rewarding to show students some of these to increase their awareness of how comparisons can enrich description of place or action. One of the most frequent metaphoric patterns in Paulsen's work comes from his love of the arts. Notice these artistic allusions from various Paulsen stories:

- In Paulsen's homage to the American family farm, *Clabbered Dirt, Sweet Grass* (1992), plowing farm fields is described as "the first great music of summer" (19).

- Wil Neuton in *The Island* (1988) takes up drawing as a way of studying and understanding what he sees on the island he has retreated to and then uses art to describe himself also: "I am a painting" (32).

- The young protagonist in *A Christmas Sonata* (1992) hears his relatives talking softly at the kitchen table while he is in bed, and their words sound to him "like a song" (55).

Additional comparisons enhance descriptive passages in other Paulsen novels:

- In describing horses in the barn, the narrator of *The Winter Room* (1989) notes that he loves to sit on their broad backs because "they are warm and gentle and somehow comfortable—like a living couch" (25).

- Remembering the woodsman Nels Thompson, Carly from *Popcorn Days and Buttermilk Nights* (1983) realizes he is "from another time in the woods when an ax wasn't just a tool but a part of a man" (60).

- As old, broken Carl from *Dancing Carl* (1983) sees Helen in town for the first time, he changes, comes alive, and "it was just like watching somebody being born" (84).

Inviting students to keep watch for metaphors and similes in prose (compared to where they usually learn about them, in poetry) enriches their awareness of what a good prose writer carries in his stylistic toolkit. Teachers might invite students to write descriptive passages using metaphors and similes after a study of Paulsen's use of them in his works.

A third stylistic fingerprint of Gary Paulsen's writing is ample use of sensory details. Paulsen's descriptions of the natural world are infused with references to sight, smell, taste, sound, and touch, and the vividness of his prose is often due to his sensory writing.

Nowhere is this more apparent than in the famous preface to *The Winter Room*, a section Paulsen titles "Tuning" as he imagines the piece to be equivalent to an orchestra warming up before performing a musical composition (Salvner 1996, 131). The section begins, "If books could be more, could show more, could own more, this book would have smells . . . ," after which he gives us some of the smells of the farmyard that serves as the book's setting: "the sweet smell of new-mown hay as it falls off the oiled sickle blade when the horses pull the mower through the field, and the sour smell of manure steaming in a winter barn" (1).

Later he asks if books can have sounds and offers some—"the high, keening sound of the six-foot bucksaws as the men pull them back and forth through the trees to cut pine for paper pulp" and "the piercing scream of the pigs when the knife cuts their throats and they know death is at hand" (2). Then he refers to the light that filters through the farm, "gold with bits of hay dust floating in it" (3), before teasing the reader with the perception that books can't have smells, sounds, or light except through readers who bring sensory experiences to the book, concluding, "The book needs you" (3).

Other Gary Paulsen novels contain vivid sensory passages:

- John Barron in *The Haymeadow* (1992) survives a terrible

mountain storm that begins with this appeal to the senses: "The first smash of thunder awakened him, seemed to come from inside his mind. It was close, so close he could smell the stink of burned air" (102).

- Sensory evocations of touch and smell come in this description from *Woodsong* (1990): "There is probably nothing that makes me feel quite as warm as coming in on a cold winter morning, leaning over the kitchen stove to warm my hands, and smelling rich pine woodsmoke and fresh bread baking in the oven" (42).

- The warming house near the Minnesota skating rinks that form the setting of *Dancing Carl* comes alive with sensory description: "In the middle of the room was a potbellied stove, black and worn, full of smoking birch with the flue open to make a small roar. The side glowed red, dull and hot. Overhead was one bulb, bare, with the hot wire showing inside" (33).

Teachers often invite students to write descriptive passages using sensory details, and models are immensely useful to shape this practice. Once again, Gary Paulsen can be a source of such models, and students might use his prose to detect patterns for piling sensory details together.

Finally, Gary Paulsen is a master of variation in sentence length, combining short, dramatic statements with sentences that string together phrases and clauses into long progressions of text to create rhythm and flow in writing. The short statements are everywhere:

- "He was stopped," Paulsen writes to capture the fear in Brian as the plane is about to crash in *Hatchet* (12).

- "He smelled the air again. Rain" (8) is how he introduces a coming storm in *The Haymeadow*.

- "We know" (92) is repeated several times in the coda entitled "Words" at the end of *Nightjohn* (1993).

Another place where these short statements appear frequently is in chapter endings, either to sum up the chapter or to propel the reader to the next. Gary Paulsen summarizes the chaotic courthouse scene when Mick Strum brings the townspeople of Bolton to his vision of their monument with the single word "Trees" (140), and he drives us into the next chapter earlier in the same book when protagonist Rocky Turner prepares to tell us about her pet dog: "I met Python" (14).

At the same time that Paulsen sometimes uses short, dramatic statements for effect in his prose, he is also the master of the running sentence, a cluster of clauses and phrases that carry on and on, creating rhythmic flow. Sometimes these contain embedded clauses or parallel constructions, sometimes they are periodic in structure, in which the sentence doesn't complete itself grammatically until the very end. Listen to these examples of undulation and melody in Paulsen's prose:

> And Erickson skating back and forth, fighting the eyes the way a northern pike fights the hook, tearing back and forth and skating around the rink, wilder and faster and faster with all of us standing and watching until finally he could stand it no more, until none of us could stand it any longer and he skate-ran to the gate and off the ice and into the warming house. (*Dancing Carl* [1983], 48)

> The plowshares come off the forge red and to the edge of white, trailing sparks, and take the hammer in dull rings to squeeze the steel back out into an edge, sharp and shiny and tight, and the horses stand, stand for their shoes while they are put hot on the hoof, held a moment in a blue swirl of smoke that stinks of burned hair and feathers, sticky sweet smoke that curls like oil in the air, before they are splashed in water to cool before nailing them on. (*Clabbered Dirt, Sweet Grass* [1992], 10)

> The water detonated, surged up at his face, and a shark's gaping
> maw, teeth flashing in the moonlight, triangular-death-razor-sharp-
> teeth, blew up and out of the darkness, slashed past his face in a rip-
> ping sideways motion, and savagely raked down the side of the hull,
> slamming against the side of the boat so hard that it knocked the
> Frog sideways. (*The Voyage of the* Frog [1989], 63)

Regardless of how the clause and phrase patterns work in these constructions, it is clear that the effect is of fluency and rhythm as the story is driven forward.

Paulsen's craft is particularly remarkable when several of these devices are yoked together. Notice the dramatic effect when he yokes short and long sentences and repetition together in this remarkable description of the last hours of a Saturday night community barn dance in *Clabbered Dirt, Sweet Grass*:

> Saturday night.
>
> Until it is late. Later than any other night and the band has
> stopped the stomping music and is doing slow waltzes for the men
> and women who truly love, truly work and truly starve and truly
> laugh and truly cry and truly love each other, for them the band
> plays slow waltzes while the children sleep in a booth and the boys
> still not men sit with girls on the steps and hold hands and touch
> arms and trade small kisses and large promises and the men and the
> women who truly love waltz with each other slowly around the
> wooden floor as if the world, the dirt, the animals, the farm, the
> luck—as if none of it were there. Just their love and the slow waltz in
> the quiet building with the wooden floors until finally, finally, the
> music stops and the children are carried to the back of the truck still
> sleeping to drive slowly, slowly home and to bed.
>
> Saturday night. (38–39)

I began this section by speculating that young adults are often not appreciative of style, but the rewards are there for teachers who draw attention to it. Young readers who react in particular ways to a story (with laughter, tears, shock) might be curious to know how a writer has produced such reactions, and an exploration into style might illuminate how. Likewise, student writers can learn a great deal about their choices as they compose by examining stylistic effects in stories they admire. This is what Meg Silver did in Chapter 3 when she invited students to study Paulsen's "brush strokes" in *The Monument*, using Harry Noden's concept from *Image Grammar* (1999).

Another stylistic lesson that bears promise is using imitation to motivate students to compose sentences and paragraphs modeled after those they had read. Stephen Dunning and William Stafford illustrate in *Getting the Knack* (1992) how this might be done in poetry writing with a series of "copy-change" exercises, and a similar sequence might be created for prose.

Imagine the results of having students copy the style even in a complex passage like the "Saturday night" quotation from *Clabbered Dirt, Sweet Grass* discussed earlier. Here is how such a passage on a student's description of the school cafeteria at lunchtime might begin:

> Monday lunch.
>   Until we are full. Fuller than any other lunch and the workers have stopped serving the pizza but are still bringing out dessert for the jocks and pretties who truly love, truly play and primp and truly laugh but never cry, truly love themselves, for them the workers hand out extra servings while the nerds huddle on corner tables. . . .

There are rewards to focusing on effective style, both to enhance students' reading and to enrich their writing, and Gary Paulsen's stylistic flourishes offer rich lessons in how style can make stories compelling and satisfying.

Paulsen the Humorist—Teaching Tone

The moods in Gary Paulsen's books range all the way from sweetness to anger, but one prominent pattern is his humor. Gary Paulsen loves to laugh and to make us laugh.

Students of virtually all ages are acclimated to mood or tone, recognizing instinctively the difference between a parent's anger and affection, or between a teacher's sternness and encouragement. Not often enough, however, are they invited to examine how tone is created in a literary work. Usually they can recognize the mood of what they're reading, but rarely are they able to analyze how a writer creates it. Gary Paulsen's humorous works are an excellent place to do so, for the laughter in his books is palpable, and the ways he creates it are relatively easy to point out.

Walter Hogan's useful work *Humor in Young Adult Literature* (2005) makes the point that, although growing up is often a serious and stressful experience for adolescents, some writers for young adults "have managed to generate humor from situations in which a protagonist experiences a major setback in some rite of passage" (182). Many of Gary Paulsen's recent works fit in this category, particularly in dramatizing puberty in boys. In *The Schernoff Discoveries* (1997) we meet Harold Schernoff and his best friend—the book's narrator—who enroll in home economics class to meet girls but are wholly inept at interactions with them. (The first chapter begins with the epigraph, "What is it anyway?" which is Harold's evaluation of the topic of sex.)

In *The Amazing Life of Birds* (2006), Gary Paulsen introduces us to Duane Homer Leech, who discovers a pimple on his forehead one morning: "Then I looked in the mirror over the sink and there was a zit in the middle of my forehead. Not just a small one. A giant. It looked like something in there was trying to get out . . ." (15).

Duane tries to squeeze the pimple, with poor results:

> Well, enough of that. But now instead of a zit I have what the TV would call a "suppurating wound." It isn't important to know what that means—just the sound of the words makes it work.
>
> I have another zit on my chest which the shirt will cover but in the mirror my face looks like I tried to kiss a rotary mower. (15–16)

Jacob Freisten in *The Boy Who Owned the School* (1990) is a ninth grader whose mother greets him every morning with the question, "Good morning—how is the boy who owns the school today?" (1) but who, like all adolescents, feels he owns and is in control of nothing, including friendships, his relationships with girls, and, of course, the dreaded gym class, presided over by the gym teacher Mr. Rocco, "who had a neck bigger than his head and seemed to know only three words: 'Gimmie a lap'" (20).

Slapstick humor also features in many Gary Paulsen books, including nearly all of the episodes in the autobiographical *How Angel Peterson Got His Name* (2003). The book's vignettes include Carl "Angel" Peterson trying to break "the world ski record" on a pair of Army surplus skis while being towed behind a car; Emil learning to hang glide with an old World War II target kite; and Orvis Orvisen getting in trouble and blaming town bully Archie Swenson for it. Even the chapter titles imply the humor of these adolescent catastrophes: "Girls, and the Circle of Death," "Orvis Orvisen and the Crash and Bash," and "And Finally, Skateboards, Bungee Jumping and Other Failures."

Paulsen's immensely popular *Harris and Me* (1993) is filled with slapstick humor as the narrator and his cousin Harris spend the summer on Harris' family's farm, getting into trouble. The character of Harris solidifies the humor in this delightful book for middle grade readers, for he's full of daring and mischief, and is both creative and impulsive—a dangerous combination as the boys try to re-create Gene Autry cowboy adventures and convert a gas-engine wringer washer into a motorized bicycle. Probably the most famous scene from the book is when Harris is dared into peeing on an electric fence, and it's Paulsen's favorite. I once heard him attempt to read the episode aloud at a publisher's reception, and his laughter was so constant and raucous that he was barely able to finish.

So what do all these humorous characters and vignettes offer to students today? First, as Walter Hogan observes in *Humor in Young Adult Literature* (2005), funny stories are disarming for students. "Humor," he notes, "can provide a teen a way of taking himself a bit less seriously, of gaining some degree of perspective on problems that at times seem overwhelming" (202). Second, humorous works offer insight into how tone is created in literature. Students reading Paulsen's comedies might be invited to catalog examples of exaggeration, slapstick, and situational humor in the stories. Putting Paulsen alongside other excellent authors of young adult literature who use humor—Joan Bauer, Terry Pratchett, Richard Peck, and Gordon Korman, for example—students might identify the events and people of our lives that lighten our worldview and make us laugh.

Patty Campbell (1999) cautions about overanalyzing humor, noting that "analyzing the rare gift of comedy is in the end as futile as dissecting a mouse to find the squeak" (363). Still, humor is a worthy topic of classroom study. A particularly promising approach is to invite students to create humorous texts rather than to analyze them. For example, teachers might give students a list of character types and familiar situations and ask them to select one to write about humorously. Not all students will be fully successful in this attempt as humor is difficult to write, but most should be able to capture funny situations, dialogue, and characters well enough to make the point about what makes for effective humor. Following is a list of possible character types and situations that might invite comedic writing from students.

Create a humorous description of one of the following character types:

- a bully

- a nerdy teacher

- a pompous cheerleader

- a confused school principal

- an arrogant school athlete

- a fussy cafeteria worker

- a clueless parent

- a lazy school custodian

Create a humorous narrative around one of these situations:

- a first date

- April Fool's Day in school

- a meal at a fast-food restaurant

- the world's worst shopping trip

- a family vacation

- a school cafeteria occurrence

- a school assembly event

Gary Paulsen's humorous writing can be an effective springboard to lessons on literary tone and effective descriptive or narrative writing. Using comedic novels lightens the tone of a class and invites students to laugh while they learn.

CHRONOLOGY

Gary Paulsen's Selected Works

2005   *The Time Hackers*
2006   *The Amazing Life of Birds*
2006   *The Legend of Bass Reeves*
2007   *Lawn Boy*
2009   *Mudshark*

Anderson, Laurie Halse. 1999. *Speak*. New York: Farrar, Straus & Giroux.

Atwell, Nancie. 1998. *In the Middle: New Understanding About Writing, Reading, and Learning*. 2d ed. Portsmouth, NH: Boynton/Cook.

———. 2002. *Lessons That Change Writers*. Portsmouth, NH: Heinemann.

———. 2007. *The Reading Zone: How to Help Kids Become Skilled, Passionate, Habitual, Critical Readers*. New York: Scholastic.

Blasingame, James B. 2007. *Gary Paulsen*. Westport, CT: Greenwood.

Brown, Jean E., and Elaine C. Stephens. 1995. *Teaching Young Adult Literature: Sharing the Connections*. Belmont, CA: Wadsworth.

Campbell, Patty. 1999. "The Sand in the Oyster: Funny Girls." *Horn Book* 75 (3 [May]): 359–63.

Daniels, Harvey. 2002. *Literature Circles: Voice and Choice in Book Clubs and Reading Groups*. 2d ed. Portland, ME: Stenhouse.

Dunning, Stephen, and William Stafford. 1992. *Getting the Knack*. Urbana, IL: National Council of Teachers of English.

Fletcher, Ralph, and JoAnn Portalupi. 2001. *Writing Workshop: The Essential Guide*. Portsmouth, NH: Heinemann.

Gerstein, Mordicai. 2003. *The Man Who Walked Between the Towers*. Brookfield, CT: Roaring Brook.

Hogan, Walter. 2005. *Humor in Young Adult Literature: A Time to Laugh*. Lanham, MD: Scarecrow.

Noden, Harry R. 1999. *Image Grammar: Using Grammatical Structures to Teach Writing*. Portsmouth, NH: Boynton/Cook.

Paulsen, Gary. 1983. *Dancing Carl*. New York: Bradbury.

———. 1983. *Popcorn Days and Buttermilk Nights*. New York: E. P. Dutton.

———. 1984. *Tracker*. New York: Bradbury.

———. 1985. *Dogsong*. New York: Bradbury.

———. 1987. *The Crossing*. New York: Orchard.

———. 1987. *Hatchet*. New York: Bradbury.

———. 1988. *The Island*. New York: Orchard.

———. 1989. *The Voyage of the* Frog. New York: Orchard.

———. 1989. *The Winter Room*. New York: Orchard.

———. 1990. *The Boy Who Owned the School*. New York: Orchard.

———. 1990. *Woodsong*. New York: Bradbury/Macmillan.

———. 1991. *The Cookcamp*. New York: Orchard.

———. 1991. *The Monument*. New York: Delacorte.

———. 1991. *The River*. New York: Delacorte.

———. 1992. *A Christmas Sonata*. New York: Delacorte.

———. 1992. *Clabbered Dirt, Sweet Grass*: New York: Harcourt Brace Jovanovich.

———. 1992. *The Haymeadow*. New York: Delacorte.

———. 1993. *Harris and Me*. New York: Harcourt Brace Jovanovich.

———. 1993. *Nightjohn*. New York: Delacorte.

———. 1993. *Sisters/Hermanas*. New York: Harcourt Brace Jovanovich.

———. 1994. *The Car*. New York: Harcourt Brace Jovanovich.

———. 1996. *Brian's Winter*. New York: Delacorte.

———. 1997. *Sarny*. New York: Delacorte.

———. 1997. *The Schernoff Discoveries*. New York: Delacorte.

———. 1999. *Alida's Song*. New York: Delacorte.

———. 1999. *Brian's Return*. New York: Delacorte.

———. 2001. *Caught by the Sea*. New York: Delacorte.

———. 2001. *Guts*. New York: Delacorte.

———. 2003. *Brian's Hunt*. New York: Wendy Lamb.

———. 2003. *How Angel Peterson Got His Name*. New York: Wendy Lamb.

———. 2004. *The Quilt*. New York: Wendy Lamb.

———. 2006. *The Amazing Life of Birds*. New York: Wendy Lamb.

———. 2008. Email correspondence to author. December 9.

Salvner, Gary M. 1996. *Presenting Gary Paulsen*. Boston: Twayne.

Stover, Lois T. 2000. "Who Am I? Who Are You? Diversity and Identity in the Young Adult Novel." In *Reading Their World: The Young Adult Novel in the Classroom*, 2d ed., ed. Virginia R. Monseau and Gary M. Salvner, 100–20. Portsmouth, NH: Boynton/Cook.

Westerfeld, Scott. 2005. *Uglies*. New York: Simon Pulse.